'Making it Happen tells some inspirational stories – from generals to GPs, and mountaineers to multinational CEOs. But from these unique stories it teaches us some profound lessons on how to execute strategy – with purpose and agility.'

Sir Graham Wrigley, co-founder partner of
Permira and Chairman of CDC Group Plc

'This book reminds us what's possible, it's compulsive reading if you want to turn dreams to reality.'

Tracy Edwards MBE

'I have always had passion for exploration, climbing new routes and going to places where no one has ever been before. It's a spirit of exploration, innovation and discovery, that's fundamental for growth in the wider world as it is in the mountains, and in the pages of this book we read fine examples of people from all walks of life who have taken initiative and changed the world for the better. It's inspirational and shows us all how with the right mindset we too can take on the mantle and make a difference.'

Sir Chris Bonington

'I thoroughly enjoyed these heroic case studies of successful strategy from a woman who knows first-hand how hard it is to reach the summit. Rebecca Stephens' insightful analysis of a refreshing array of organizations from the arts, government and healthcare to outer space inspires us with well-told tales of surprisingly down-to-earth yet visionary leaders who took that crucial step toward Making it Happen.'

Dr Dina Dommett, Ashridge Dean,
Hult International Business School

REBECCA STEPHENS

MAKING

it

HAPPEN

Lessons from the Frontline
of Strategy Execution

BLOOMSBURY

BLOOMSBURY BUSINESS
Bloomsbury Publishing Plc
50 Bedford Square, London, WC1B 3DP, UK
29 Earlsfort Terrace, Dublin 2, Ireland

BLOOMSBURY, BLOOMSBURY BUSINESS and the Diana logo are trademarks
of Bloomsbury Publishing Plc

First published in Great Britain 2021

A catalogue record for this book is available from the British Library

Library of Congress Cataloging-in-Publication data has been applied for

ISBN: HB: 978-1-4729-9204-8; eBook: 978-1-4729-9205-5

2 4 6 8 10 9 7 5 3 1

Typeset by Deanta Global Publishing Services, Chennai, India
Printed and bound in Great Britain by CPI Group (UK) Ltd, Croydon CR0 4YY

To find out more about our authors and books visit www.bloomsbury.com
and sign up for our newsletters

Contents

Preface

by Tony Renton, Chairman of a number
of technology start-up companies

Life throws up challenges and people rise to meet them, and they find solutions. They have done so through the millennia and will continue to do so in the future; it is the very nature of human beings. Naturally, every generation thinks it has a harder time of it than the last, but this one might have more cause to think so than most. The sheer weight of numbers of us as human beings, a planet visibly creaking under the strain, an endless turnover of ideological and religious conflicts, threats unseen in the shape of viruses and cyber warfare, and a global debt approaching $300 trillion. Now, more than ever, each of us needs to step forward and play our part to address the challenges we face.

From my own experience in business, I know that to find a way and implement a strategy to make things happen isn't always easy. It requires clarity, energy, and sticking power. So, it is wonderfully inspiring to read in the pages of this book about remarkable men and women who have repeatedly found ways to influence and shape their worlds for the better. They are all realists. They look at the world as it is – good and bad – and refuse to allow themselves to be daunted by circumstance or the magnitude of the challenge. Contributors to this book could see that the NHS was in a state of chronic ill-health; that people were starving on the streets of Sarajevo; that London kids weren't getting the education they deserved, and for them, this was a call to action. It wasn't somebody else's problem to sort out, it was theirs. Through a strong sense of purpose and commitment to the cause, great leadership and communication skills, they determinedly executed strategies to turn the situations around.

In my own field, oil and gas, two young men working for the Norwegian energy giant Equinor looked at their own industry and acknowledged that it wasn't sustainable in the long term and took the first baby steps to transformation through digitalization, improving efficiencies and paving the way for a shift towards renewables in the future. They have helped not only their own company but the sector as a whole.

Without exception, the contributors to this book were optimistic that solutions could be found, regardless of the difficulty of the task.

For many years, I was a commercial director at BP with responsibilities across the Middle East. BP is a complex global business and like Equinor and other energy companies, it is challenged by the need to plan beyond the horizon. The dilemma now is can oil companies transform themselves into energy companies to meet the climate challenge? Do they have the requisite skills? Much inward thinking is going on – how will renewables compete for capital, will the funds that own shares be confident in their future dividends, and so on. Strategies for this transformation are emerging – it's as much a revolution as evolution. The companies have well-developed capabilities to do this, but strategy on its own isn't enough – it needs to be combined with people who take decisive action and are not afraid to take calculated risks. It's rare in my experience to find someone who is good at both, but having both skills in one's team is, to me, a pre-requisite for success. I reflect on the leadership style of those in this book – all highly effective, but each different. There is so much within these pages for the reader to learn from their wealth of experiences and different styles of leadership.

When I look at my own style I believe, or would like to believe, it is open, collegiate, occasionally firm, listening, trusting, team-based and optimistic. What gives me the most pleasure is recognizing and utilizing exceptional talent. Whilst I'm a big fan of team-based delivery I recognize that there are along the way 'but for me' moments where someone really stands out either with exceptional delivery or with a light-bulb moment idea; I need to give space to allow and encourage this to happen.

On the wheel of management styles, I come out more as a strategic architect and weaker on the concluder/producer aspects of delivery, so over the years I have ensured I bridge my own weaknesses by bringing in others with diverse style and skills. While acknowledging that there are continuing advancements in technology and an array of methods and processes to call upon to facilitate implementation, the fact remains that the differentiator between tick-box implementation and exemplary implementation is how we work together with people. Working well within our own teams and with those outside is not only crucial – it makes work fun and rewarding. During the pandemic it is surely the ability to sit down with others and map the way forward that we all missed.

Since leaving BP I have set up and sold a consultancy and was co-founder of an energy company. Now, as Non-Exec Chairman of several young companies such as OGL Geothermal, Airponix, S-Cube, EPEX, as well as being one of the founders of the charity Saving India's Tigers, I look to ensure balanced teams. I've realized that it's better to back a good team with a bad plan than vice-versa – a good team will soon ditch a bad plan and develop a good plan and make it happen. I like the quiet achievers, those that under-promise and over-deliver, and I note that every person featured in this book over-delivers by quite some margin. One of the areas where I feel things could still improve is in finding and holding onto simplicity in complexity – so still lots to work on.

I took away something from each of the remarkable stories and am sure any reader will find something to inspire them and help in the challenges they face. There is the principled leadership of General Sir Michael Rose, the palpable energy and courage of Tamara Rojo, and the dogged determination and exemplary 100 per cent commitment to performing to one's absolute best of the mountaineer Nimsdai Purja.

I hadn't heard the story of Krystyna Skarbek; how one woman could achieve so much in the most testing of circumstances. Her positive mindset, commitment and courage must surely give a nudge to anyone thinking they might not be able to make a difference amidst all the issues and global challenges we face in the world today. I came away from reading the book with renewed hope and trusting we have so many more people like those portrayed in the book that will step up to the plate. My wish is that, like Krystyna, their response to the clarion call will be 'I can help'.

Acknowledgements

The following people gave generously of their time, and imparted their wisdom so that I might capture it, at least in part, in the pages of this book. I was transfixed as each told me their story in their studio, clinic, classroom, office or comfort of their own home – or latterly, over Zoom. I thank each one of them, too, for kindly answering questions and providing clarification to ensure accuracy. They are: Emma Bridgewater, John Clarke, Dr Peter Robbins, Simon Pulsford, Tim Wright, Jens Festervoll, Stein Petter Aannerud, Dr James Morrow, Dr Laurence Kemp, General Sir Michael Rose, Dame Helena Morrissey, Tamara Rojo, Sir David Wright, William Allen, Nimsdai Purja, Sir Tim Brighouse, Sir Anthony Seldon, Neil and Jane Lunnon, Ian Morris and Gideon Heugh.

Many others have added depth and colour to the stories, or generously provided direction and ideas, checked facts and data, and generally supported the book from its inception through to its publication. They include Tamara Box, Lieutenant-General Sir Graeme Lamb, Dr Peter Robbins, Zubair Ahmed, Sabina Horga, Charles Antelme, Dan Phelan, Oliver Szasz, Charlotte Southwell and Betony Baylis. I thank NASA for kindly agreeing to William Allen telling his part of the story of the Artemis programme. Thanks also to Clare Grist Taylor who knocked the proposal into shape, Matt James of Bloomsbury for taking it on, and Allie Collins and Harriet Power for being such brilliant, sympathetic editors. Thanks also to Jasmine Parker for the cover design, Rachel Murphy in production, Amy Greaves in publicity and Rosie Parnham in marketing – an altogether professional Bloomsbury team. And, of course, Paul Heugh, who is not only a contributor of this book, but whose idea it was, and who has been the support every writer needs from start to finish.

Introduction

This book is for people who want to make things happen – who want to make a difference in the world – and yet feel incredibly frustrated at just how difficult that can sometimes be. Bureaucracy, complexity and a no-can-do attitude so often seem to be obstacles in our path that we might be forgiven for settling for something less than we had hoped for or aspired to achieve.

And yet there are exceptions. There are individuals who through their sense of purpose, through their conviction and optimism, through an uncommon commitment, and through their skill at bringing out the very best in those around them, accomplish extraordinary things to the benefit of themselves and other people, and to society at large. This book tells the stories of a dozen or so such individuals, from different walks of life, who by their own admission might consider themselves less than perfect but who nonetheless have been tremendously successful at implementing strategies in sectors as diverse as the military, the arts, medicine, mountaineering, the oil and gas industry, the civil service, education, business, retail and space exploration. We tell their stories here in the hope that we can learn from their experiences and be inspired to implement strategy more effectively.

This book was conceived by Paul Heugh, a man for whom implementing strategy is a passion unto itself and who has a healthy track record of making things happen, both in business and in his earlier career in the military. Heugh has led a life that has been dedicated to leading and delivering difficult projects. His formative years in the army shaped his thinking and belief toward the completion of the task – that thinking creatively, a refusal to give up and going the extra mile is an absolute state of being. And then he went on to work in one of the world's top global organizations, GlaxoSmithKline (GSK), for over 20 years, and for the majority of this time was dedicated to strategy execution.

At GSK, Heugh was recognized for his rare ability to organize, plan and lead projects that crossed the traditional lines within the organization. Special roles were repeatedly created for him to take on yet another big challenge, each time expanding his geographical and functional remit. He served on the global leadership team, tackling everything from new product launches and business turnarounds to functional and geographical transformations and global capability building. He built a diverse and highly respected global strategic projects team that was sought after across the company for its ability to manage the complex and difficult. And he personally trained, mentored and coached hundreds of employees, sharing his insights on how to lead and manage without traditional line authority but across a matrix. Such was his reputation that few would consider taking on a new challenge without the support of one of his team.

But in 2012, it was time to move on. Heugh had long wanted to share his amassed knowledge and experience with others and created a boutique consultancy to do just that. This consultancy, Skarbek Associates, specializes in the key success factor of any organization or business: the *implementation* of strategy (although he knows the importance of defining a strategy as well). It blends the best of everything Heugh learned from the military and business worlds with the knowledge and skills of a highly diverse and dedicated team.

I first met Paul Heugh some 20 years ago when he invited me to talk to his colleagues at GSK about climbing Everest. Paul is a mountaineer himself so it was a subject that naturally interested him. But the real value of the talk was in the lessons drawn from the leadership and teamwork on an expedition at extreme altitude that were equally valid for project management teams operating in the demanding and often high-pressure corporate arena. Paul had long recognized the value of story-telling as a learning tool and invited me back to relay stories from Everest and also the climbing of the Seven Summits, the highest mountain on each of the seven continents. The idea was to bring to life the human skills that support the different stages of the project life cycle – initiation, planning, execution and control, and completion – for his in-house project management training programme. Today, I continue to work with Paul as a consultant at Skarbek Associates.

When Paul first hatched his plan to write a book on strategy execution, I could see the value of it immediately and it didn't take me very long to be persuaded to be the scribe. Working alongside Paul, it was obvious that this was a subject about which he had a rare, comprehensive and deep understanding that would be of value to a wider audience than he could reach through his consultancy. I also wholly approved of the story-telling approach he wanted to adopt, believing this far more memorable and thus informative than any number of models, graphs and pie charts.

There are many books purporting to unlock a success formula for implementing strategies and managing projects. The difference with this book is its emphasis on the power that every one of us has within us to make a difference in the world. Some might find themselves doubting this is possible, but read the stories in this book and you will see that time and time again it is one individual that is the catalyst to change. It is very often an individual's mindset that is the driver of success, and with hard work, dedication and commitment, they make things happen. This is a book that offers hope, as well as guidance. Within the narrative of each chapter there are valuable insights for strategy execution whatever your industry or role may be. The book shines a light on essential factors – organization, process, tools and techniques – that require constant attention if excellent execution of strategy is to be achieved.

The fundamental premise of this book is that the vast majority of organizations can implement strategy far better than they are currently doing, and that each one of us can personally make a significant contribution. This empowerment of the individual –

not allowing ourselves to be overwhelmed with what might seem a hopeless battle against the corporation, the multinational or the state – is magnificently embodied in a single woman in whose honour Heugh chose to name his consultancy: the Polish countess, Krystyna Skarbek.

Many consider Countess Krystyna Skarbek (aka Christine Granville) to have influenced the Second World War in Britain's favour more than any other woman, and she was regarded as Churchill's favourite spy. But why? And how? Put simply, it was a personal drive and a belief that she could do something to help. Her outrage that the Nazis should be occupying her country led her to England and then, after meeting an MI6 agent in London, to signing up to the Secret Intelligence Service. She was driven to action and submitted a bold plan to ski into Nazi-occupied Poland across the Carpathian Mountains in winter. The report on her actions said 'she is absolutely fearless'. Though shot at, chased and captured, she escaped and successfully created an escape line across the mountains, through which she aided the passage of several hundred Polish pilots who would later go on to play a decisive role in the Battle of Britain.

While Krystyna Skarbek operated in a cataclysmic period of conflict and accelerated technological, economic and societal change, it can be argued that we are living through a comparable state of upheaval today. That our times are challenging, there is no doubt. Things that once seemed permanent are proving not to be. We live in an age where the balance of nation states is shifting, and the heady mix of technological advances, population growth and movement, along with the dramatic effects of climate change, has added to a sense of angst as to what the future may hold. This uncertain landscape is matched in the commercial world, where risks to old models and opportunities for new ones abound. Change – in the sense of an initiative that is implemented and then at some concrete point finishes – is a thing of the past. Today change is a constant, and one that isn't about to slow, but rather increase in pace exponentially.

To grasp the pace of change today, and in the near future, take for example automation. A World Economic Forum report published in April 2021 forecasts that the rate of automation is increasing at such a pace that the division of labour as a share of hours spent will be 47 per cent machine to 53 per cent human as early as in 2025, compared with 33 per cent machine and 67 per cent human in 2020. This is a seismic shift. Meanwhile, we are managing an explosion in information technology that is simultaneously mind-blowing and crushing in its unprecedented volumes of data and new information systems to assimilate. Customer demands are only increasing, as is regulation. There is repeated restructuring of organizations, mergers and acquisitions. Companies run across international lines with workforces turning over apace and an ever-present need to do more with less. What was complicated became complex; the complexity intensified and now borders on chaos.

The fallout from such intense complexity is that the gap between intent and delivery, between strategy and its execution, is widening in such a way that initiatives and projects fail or are all too often sub-optimal. This is true across all sectors, both public and private. The shortfall can prove both expensive and damaging for organizations, and is negative for the economy.

Talk to people in organizations across the board and the majority will admit that implementing strategy is difficult – and research data backs up their concerns. The PMI's 2020 edition of *Pulse of the Profession* highlights feedback from over 3,000 project professionals from around the globe and spans a range of industries, including information technology, financial service, government, manufacturing, energy, construction, healthcare and telecom. It reveals that while 69 per cent of projects broadly meet goals and business intent, projects often fail to meet the two key objectives of project management – time and budget. At 47 per cent, almost half the projects were delivered late, and 41 per cent were over budget. A further 13 per cent of projects were deemed failures.

Mathematics of Mediocrity

It is the majority of projects and initiatives – those that are neither outright successes or failures but which sit somewhere in the middle, being late, over budget or short on quality – that Skarbek feels can benefit most from improved strategy implementation. The consultancy even has a term for it – the **Zone of Mediocrity** – where leaked value can be considerable and, when made apparent, can be a catalyst for an organization with ambition to clamber up and out as fast as possible.

Organizations might be driven to do this even more quickly when they look at what Skarbek calls the **Mathematics of Mediocrity**. The fact is that usually, when a project is struggling, the cost of its failure is couched only in terms of the project budget: 'We've sunk £20m into this initiative and we're still not finished.' But unfortunately the actual costs are far greater. An accurate picture isn't drawn until one factors in the consequential losses as well – the delay in starting the next project, for example, or a one-off marketing opportunity that's been lost. When these costs are factored in, Skarbek has seen lost value and oncosts totalling up to a staggering 9.5 times the declared project costs. That turns a struggling £20m project into a disastrous £190m failure.

The complexity of our world is undoubtedly one of the reasons that implementing strategies is so difficult, but there are other reasons too. An important factor is the evolution of the matrix multinational as a widely prevalent business and organizational model. There was a time when there was a comforting sense of order within organizations, in the shape of functions and divisional silos. Today it's commonplace for companies to operate cross-functional teams with multiple projects and initiatives competing for people's time and effort. The challenges of working collaboratively across such a matrix without line authority are acute, and only amplified when interacting beyond the border of a firm with suppliers and agencies who are operating with different priorities.

Add to this a more transient workforce, with people shifting jobs within and outside the organization, and we start to see some of the challenges. As an example, Heugh worked on a retrospective review of a project with a business leader who was astounded to discover there had been nine changes of project leader in the three years of the project's life cycle. We might call a group of people a team, but are they actually so, with players committed to a common goal and holding themselves mutually accountable? Or are the changes in personnel so frequent, the geography so distant, and the conflicting demands on individuals so great, that actually they are a disparate group of people with differing values, frames of reference and agendas?

Yet another challenge is the inability or unwillingness to prioritize, sometimes driven by fear that an initiative or project that isn't ranked as a priority might nonetheless yield results. Such spread betting of projects is rife in companies seeking to grow through innovation, and all too often the unforeseen consequence is sluggishness across the whole organization.

However, despite gloomy figures and the very real challenges that we face on a day-to-day basis, there is reason to be optimistic. An awareness of the problem is of course the first step, and with the right attitude and know-how, marked improvements in efficiency most definitely can be made. Even in organizations that might be considered to function perfectly well, every incremental percentage point of added efficiency can result in a significant material advantage. So this book is a call for action, to focus on and build capability in the *implementation* of strategy in schools, universities, hospitals, in the military and government, in NGOs and in businesses, so there is less wastage and greater productivity for the benefit of us all.

It is also a book that embraces a breadth of experience in successfully implementing strategy in many different worlds. It shows a diversity of styles, backgrounds and approaches to implementing strategy – all equally valid, and from which we can all learn. The individuals featured in this book might all be regarded as heroic in their own particular fields. Each one of them exhibits courage: the courage to be different and stand apart from the group, to have conviction and lead others to implement what they believe to be the best way forward. They are bearers of intangible qualities that resonate throughout their stories; qualities that can be described with words such as *ethos, culture, energy, belief, passion, determination, doggedness, resilience, accuracy, imagination, communication* and importantly in this exponentially fast-changing world of ours, *agility* – the ability to constantly be on their toes, to skip this way or that in response to rapidly evolving circumstances, to pivot and to seize new opportunities.

And then there is the more easily definable 'process' to achieve success – the fundamentals to succeeding in any walk of life that are constant. These might be the responsibility of leaders to craft a vision, to build both alignment to it and the team to deliver it, and then to actually ensure execution. Heugh maintains that a combination of industry expertise together with a golden thread of military DNA is remarkably effective in finding the route to successful strategy implementation. It is from a martial tradition that he expands on the basic model of vision, alignment and execution, and finds the following markers useful in navigating the journey to effective strategy execution:

- Decide what it is you want to achieve. Agree and align on a vision and strategy.
- With a thorough understanding of the context, risks and opportunities, examine the alternative methods to implementing the strategy and thoroughly test them. Consider the bold and unusual – think the unthinkable.

- Gather together people with the right expertise to plan the execution at both a macro and micro level.
- Trust people to deliver your plans by guiding, helping and occasionally driving.
- Always keep one eye on the horizon for the next inevitable change and be prepared to adjust your finely crafted plans accordingly.

This last point – to be agile, to be fluid, to be able to respond quickly to changes in the internal and external environment without losing momentum or vision – is an increasingly crucial skill and a core differentiator in today's rapidly changing business environment. Krystyna Skarbek was an exemplar of quick wittedness in the field. As just one example, in August 1944, she heard that fellow SOE agent and senior leader in the resistance movement in France, Francis Cammaerts, had been captured along with two other people and was being held by the Gestapo. She promptly marched into the Gestapo HQ claiming to be the niece of Field Marshal Montgomery. She spun a story that instilled fear in the captors and in doing so secured her colleagues' release and their lives.

Contributors to this book also display such agility. In a quest to reinvent contemporary ballet, newly appointed artistic director of the English National Ballet, Tamara Rojo, immediately shakes things up by appointing four new ballet masters from Japan, Cuba, Spain and China. Jens Festervoll and Stein Petter Aannerud – two young employees of the Norwegian state-owned oil and gas company Equinor – grasp the digital mantle and use their combined wit and persuasive powers to form a small, disruptive and innovative group within the company, and in doing so steer the company toward a more efficient, profitable and environmentally sustainable future.

But before we read the stories of how our contributors managed to successfully overcome the odds and 'get it done', it's worth exploring in more detail the journey from strategy to execution.

What is strategy?

A common understanding of the term 'strategy' must be the starting point for anybody, or any organization, wishing to *implement* strategy. The word originates from the Greek *stratēgia*, meaning 'the art of the general', and includes a plethora of skills such as tactics, siege craft and logistics, and the art of utilizing them together to win.

While some of the more military-specific terms may not translate directly into business, the overarching definition of strategy most certainly does when viewed as a long-term plan of action designed to bring all of the component parts together in time and space to achieve a particular objective. And as in war, so in business are an organization's best-laid plans subjected to the vagaries of the social, technological, economic and climatic environments, and the actions of its competitors.

Indeed, the world we live in today may be regarded as so complex and so fast-changing that as quickly as a strategy is written, it may be rendered redundant. Which leads to a school of thought that it may be better not to write a strategy at all; better to have an 'emergent strategy' that constantly flexes and adapts to changing circumstances. But this approach carries a risk as well: that without the analytic input of writing a strategy, there will be no clearly defined path to success. Better to have a strategy but be constantly on alert to circumstantial changes in technology, innovation, the environment, population and world order. Repeatedly ask yourself the question, 'Has the situation changed?' and adapt accordingly. There lies opportunity as well as obstacles to overcome.

But back to the term 'strategy' – it is one frequently banded about, often used loosely and imprecisely with less than desirable consequences in business. The following three examples illustrate in turn the dynamism, the complexity, and paradoxically the simplicity of strategy when distilled to a straightforward formula that connects 'the end' (accomplishment of the set goal) with the 'means and ways' of achieving 'the end'. These examples can help us understand the term before exploring how best to implement strategy in organizations.

Sailing (dynamism)

First, let's draw an analogy from the world of sailing. Strategy might be described as the journey that you imagine, the route you chart, the course you steer, and the voyage that you actually make. So for example, you may decide to sail across the Atlantic Ocean. You chart your route and you set sail. It may be that you sail the course that you actually charted, but the chances are that you will sail a different route, one slightly to the north or slightly to the south, depending on the winds and the currents. And you will adjust your course as you go along, in order to ensure that you still reach the intended point on a continent on the other side of the ocean.

The point here is that strategy is dynamic. It can't be static because it takes place in time and space, and factors in time and space are constantly changing. It may be that circumstances change to such a degree that you decide to re-plot your course altogether. The Norwegian polar explorer Roald Amundsen springs to mind as an example. His original intention had been to sail north to explore the North Pole basin, but on hearing that Britain's Captain Scott was heading south in the hope of being the first to reach the South Pole, he changed his course 180 degrees and raced south instead, planting a flag at the South Pole on 14 December 1911, a full month before Captain Scott and his companions arrived, deflated, on 17 January 1912.

In an ever-changing world, adjusting or even re-plotting one's course for a bigger prize can be considered strategic. If, however, your intention is to sail the Atlantic Ocean and you hear news of a party in the Azores and decide to redirect your course in order not to miss out, that isn't a strategy, it's a distraction.

Military invasion (complexity)

Our second example – that of Napoleon and the French invasion of Russia in 1812 – illustrates the complexity of strategy and how it requires the organization and co-ordination of many interdependent factors to achieve a specific goal (in this case the defeat of the Russian army). It isn't just a single piece of the jigsaw puzzle, but the assembly of the complete picture. This story also illustrates the perils of continuing to pursue a strategy even when the situation has changed and the strategy is no longer able to achieve its intent.

Known in France as the *Russian Campaign* and in Russia as the *Patriotic War of 1812*, Napoleon's invasion of Russia has been studied by military historians through the centuries as a classic example of strategy, and indeed of how things can so easily go wrong. Russia had upset Napoleon by withdrawing from a French-led embargo against trading with Britain, and meanwhile the Russian Tsar Alexander was concerned by the formation of the Grand Duchy of Warsaw to the south. On 24 June 1812, Napoleon's *Grande Armée*, numbering somewhere between 420,000 and up to 600,000 soldiers – the largest army ever assembled in the history of warfare up until that point – crossed the Neman River with the objective of engaging and defeating the Russian army in what Napoleon hoped would be a quick, decisive victory, to secure Poland from the threat of a Russian invasion and to force the tsar to cease trading with Britain.

Napoleon's objective was a monumental logistical exercise. His army was massive and to form it, Napoleon assembled troops not just from across France but from Allied invasion forces as well. He put together a fantastic logistics machinery to equip the army. He made plans for the men to be fed, watered and sheltered on what would be an extended march through a foreign land. Napoleon had a master plan that would bring together 600,000 people to cross the Neman River and pursue the Russian army, defeating them in a big set-piece battle. He had in every sense of the word a strategy to pull together all the component parts – the men, the horses, the armoury, the intelligence – and defeat the Russians. It is an extraordinary example of the complexity of strategic planning, but it is also an example of what can go terribly wrong if shifting circumstances are ignored.

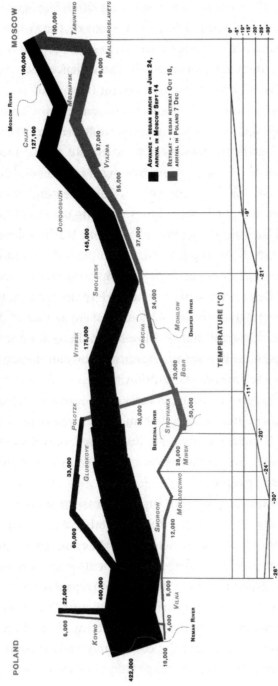

NAPOLEON'S RUSSIAN CAMPAIGN OF 1812-1813

THIS FIGURATIVE MAP, ADAPTED FROM ORIGINAL DRAWN BY RETIRED INSPECTOR GENERAL CHARLES MINARD, IN 1869, ILLUSTRATES THE SUCCESSIVE LOSSES IN MEN OF NAPOLEON'S GRAND ARMÉE IN THE RUSSIAN CAMPAIGN 1812-13. THE DARK LINE REPRESENTS NAPOLEON'S JOURNEY TO MOSCOW AND THE LIGHT GREY LINE, HIS RETREAT. THE THICKNESS OF THE LINE REPRESENTS THE NUMBER OF TROOPS; AT THE BEGINNING, UPWARDS OF 400,000 SOLDIERS, AND AT THE END, SOME 10,000. THE BOTTOM LINE ILLUSTRATES THE TEMPERATURE ON NAPOLEON'S RETREAT FROM MOSCOW, CONSISTENTLY BELOW ZERO AND AT TIMES DIPPING AS LOW AS -30 DEGREES.

In the event, the *Grande Armée* made significant progress into the interior of Russia, winning a few skirmishes en route, but it wasn't long before Napoleon's strategy started to unravel. Erratic weather conditions and frequent storms made the advance difficult. Supply wagons struggled on muddy tracks, while the troops suffered sunstroke and succumbed to disease in the heat and humidity. Meanwhile the enemy was playing a very different game from the one Napoleon had supposed, and Napoleon was slow to see it. The Russians, though vastly outnumbered by the French, were drawing Napoleon and his troops further into Russia through the very act of retreating. While doing so, they adopted scorched earth tactics, burning down villages, towns and crops and making it increasingly difficult for Napoleon to feed his advancing army. Nonetheless, Napoleon pushed on and in a little under three months he and his depleted army reached Moscow, only to discover it had been evacuated. Any hopes Napoleon may have had of agreeing a peace treaty with Tsar Alexander were dashed.

Napoleon led his army out of Moscow at the end of October, as the harsh Russian winter set in. Temperatures plummeted. Lack of food and fodder for the horses, hypothermia from the bitter cold and persistent attacks from Russian peasants and Cossacks led to great loss of life, and a general loss of discipline and cohesion in the army. By the time the last of Napoleon's troops left Russian soil, only 27,000 effective soldiers remained; the *Grande Armée* had left behind some 400,000 men, either dead or captured.

With the wonderful gift of hindsight it is easy to see that Napoleon had a clear strategy to defeat the Russians and return triumphant, and that his failure was to overlook factors that were changing around him: essentially, the enemy employing a different strategy than the one he had anticipated. Napoleon was marching with his men and would have watched this deteriorating scenario play out before his eyes. We can only speculate about the nature of his thinking. Maybe he believed the Russians were just around the corner and that his *Grande Armée* would surely defeat them in the next battle. Or maybe it was hubris on his part. Whatever his reasons, the same errors are frequently made in business. In today's climate of extreme and accelerating change, the lessons from Napoleon's failed *Russian Campaign* is that strategists need to be more watchful and agile than ever. We must resist locking ourselves into a course of action with slavish obedience but instead constantly ask ourselves, has the situation changed? And be prepared to adjust our plans accordingly.

Journey to the moon ('ends, ways and means')

Our third example illustrates how an extraordinarily complex challenge might be distilled to a remarkably simple formula of 'ends, ways and means' from which a strategy can be deduced – in this case, putting man on the moon. The formula invites the strategist to ensure the appropriate *means* are available to achieve the *ends* (or goals), with the *ways* being the path connecting them.

There can be few finer examples of an audacious and crystal-clear goal than to put the first ever human being on the moon. On 25 May 1961, President John F Kennedy addressed the US Congress on urgent national needs. 'I believe,' he declared, 'that this nation should commit itself to achieving the goal, before this decade is out, of landing a man on the moon and returning him safely to the Earth.' He continued, 'No single space project in this period will be more impressive to mankind, or more important for the long-range exploration of space; and none will be so difficult or expensive to accomplish.'

True, the knowledge to accomplish such a goal wasn't yet within man's grasp. True, the technology had yet to be developed. But crucially, the vision and intent were clear from the start, and there was total commitment to the project. This was at a critical time in the Cold War and it was clear, and universally understood, that this wasn't just a challenging technical nut to crack but a matter of national importance: both for the Americans to achieve pre-eminence over the Soviet Union in the space race, and to ingrain the supremacy of democratic freedom over communism in the eyes of the world.

The 'means' to undertake this phenomenal challenge was money from the public purse (John F Kennedy reached out to Congress for funds above and beyond the increases asked for earlier space activities), and the National Aeronautics and Space Administration (NASA), which was the governing and co-ordinating mechanism that would make it happen.

NASA personnel realized that much of the research would be experimental and that inevitably things would go wrong (which, as we know, they did). Few people alive at the time will forget the flash fire that swept through the command module of Apollo 1 during a launch rehearsal test at Cape Kennedy Air Force Station Launch Complex on 27 January 1967, killing all three pilots. NASA immediately convened its Accident Review Board to determine the cause, and it was through thorough examination of its mistakes that it continued to learn.

The 'ways' to ultimate success were through a programme approach – it was Apollo 11 that finally delivered Neil Armstrong and Buzz Aldrin to the moon on 20 July 1969, just over eight years after JFK broadcast his vision – and the creation of a collaborative organization with multiple contributors working with complete transparency and the sharing of knowledge and ideas. It was acknowledged at the start that this challenge was beyond the capabilities of a single organization, so many were pulled in – Boeing, McDonnell Douglas, Northrop Grumman and others. In total, there were 40,000 manufacturers and 2 million parts.

As Neil Armstrong broadcast to the world from Apollo 11: 'The responsibility for this flight lies first with history and with the giants of science who have preceded this effort; next with the American people, who have, through their will, indicated their desire; next with four administrations and their Congresses, for implementing that will; and then, with the agency and industry teams that built our spacecraft, the Saturn, the Columbia, the Eagle, and the little EMU, the spacesuit and backpack that was our small spacecraft out on the lunar surface.'

None of it would have been possible without defining the 'end' first: clear, bold and inspiring. Then the 'means' needed to be made available in order for NASA to put in place the 'ways' to success.

One of the major issues that organizations commonly face today is a lack of clarity. There might be a confused idea of what a vision actually is – or what *their* vision is – and the term 'strategy' might be used all too loosely. One fundamental part of the strategy equation that is repeatedly overlooked, and often not even considered, is to answer the question: *how will we win?* If a strategy doesn't tell you how you will win, then it isn't a strategy. It defies the very meaning of the term.

Back to our example of Napoleon. He had a strategy. Unfortunately for him, so did the Russians. Neither Napoleon nor the Russians had a strategy to lose; they both had strategies to win. It was just that one was better than the other. Yet in the business world, organizations talk about strategy and frequently invest a lot of money, time and effort into formulating one, while failing to address this fundamental question: *how will we win?* Or, put another way – because, unlike war, not every situation in business is competitive – *how will we thrive?* It isn't enough to *define* what you want to do and where you want to be. It is essential to identify what it is that will *enable you* to do what you want to do and be where you want to be. What will the factors at play be and how will they interact with each other to enable you to thrive?

One last point before we enjoy the stories of strategy implementation featured in this book, and that is the importance of diversity of thought. Those with a healthy growth mindset will understand there is always more to be learned and a new, better approach to solving an issue. But it would be fair to say that there's a danger, observed in some professions, that a specialist vocational education can result in a sort of blindness to the usefulness of learning from sectors other than one's own.

We passionately disagree with such isolationist thinking. In our view, the more diversity of thinking the better, and thus in this book we have chosen very deliberately to look at an eclectic mix of individuals who have been tremendously successful at implementing strategies in a diverse array of sectors that include the military, the arts, mountaineering, medicine, the oil and gas industry, the civil service, education, finance, retail, business and space exploration. Approached in this way, the writing of the book has served to highlight enduring truths that transcend sectors, but also observes nuanced differences practised by different individuals in different walks of life. It amplifies the importance of some factors in the implementation of strategy that we intuitively acknowledge as important, which are so often to do with the character and mindset of the individual – such as confidence that they can indeed make a difference, an unusually high level of commitment, a sense of purpose and utter belief in their mission, and a dogged persistence to get the job done.

There are enduring truths that also run through what might be regarded as the process of implementing strategy – for example, a clearly defined vision, focus and simplification, prioritization of that which is most important, the writing of a plan, the willingness to adapt quickly with changing circumstances and to pivot and seize opportunities, and, crucially, communication. But here we see more nuanced differences in the manifestation of these practices and plenty of opportunity to learn from our exemplars' different approaches.

Take for example communication skills. Whether or not the ability to communicate comes naturally, it is undoubtedly essential for the successful execution of strategy. Within an organization, it means repeating the message again and again and cascading it so that every player in the team understands in which direction he or she is pulling and to what end. And outside the organization, how can anybody know about your product or service unless you tell them?

Here we see very different approaches. For instance, one can't help feeling that General Sir Michael Rose would have been far happier just getting on with his job as Commander of the UN Protection Force in Bosnia without having to bother with the media at all, but he understood that he had little choice. Indeed, dealing with the media was a critical part of his job in order to win the support of the international community. So, rather than keeping journalists at arm's length, he broke with convention and invited them into the UN headquarters so they could work alongside each other and the journalists could have a chance of reporting something nearer the truth than they would have done otherwise. On the other hand, Sir Anthony Seldon, headmaster of Wellington College, positively revelled in selling his message of happiness and well-being in schools 'to the widest audience possible', and very successfully put Wellington College squarely back on the map, voted by readers of the upmarket magazine *Tatler* as the 'best senior school in Britain'.

Thus this book is not written with a view that medics skip straight to the chapter on implementing strategy in medicine, or that soldiers read only about General Sir Michael Rose. Quite the contrary. We live in extraordinary times of unprecedented change, and even the most conservative among us understand that we need to be thinking differently – more creatively – to crack some of the issues that we face both globally and closer to home in the workplace.

Skarbek brings diversity of thought to a situation by looking through multiple lenses, by drawing on the considerable and very different experiences of its staff. This book adds more lenses still. It looks at implementing strategy through the eyes of exemplary figures in the military, civil service, education, the arts, medicine, mountaineering, space exploration and finance and business – both corporates and entrepreneurs. It aims to be inspirational and to encourage you not to give up at the first hurdle but to know that you really do have it within you to make a difference – and to celebrate that we can learn from one another.

CHAPTER ONE

Fixing the National Health Service Bottom Up

If you have health, you probably will be happy, and if you have health and happiness, you have all the wealth you need, even if it is not all you want.

Elbert Hubbard, writer, artist and philosopher

The National Health Service (NHS) might hold a place deep in the psyche of virtually every Briton, but that doesn't make it the first port of call if you're looking for exemplary management and strategy implementation. Quite the opposite. Which is why a general practice in Cambridgeshire acclaimed by a former editor of *The BMJ* as 'an island of excellence and innovation surrounded by a struggling system' is worthy of a closer look.

At the time of writing, Granta Medical Practices serves 45,000 patients in five buildings, delivering in excess of 230,000 consultations per annum over a practice area of 25 by 10 miles of rural South Cambridgeshire. The Care Quality Commission rates it 'outstanding'. Patients consistently give positive feedback and general practitioners (GPs) are queuing up to work there. It is becoming a model for the evolution of local healthcare, shaping and influencing the health system around it, and yet it has had no additional resourcing whatsoever. It is on the same national contract as every other GP practice in the country.

How Granta Medical Practices started

The story starts over a decade ago with the GP Dr James Morrow. With some 12 years' experience in general practice, Dr Morrow was determined that he and his fellow practitioners should have greater influence over the future of the primary care service in the UK. 'This wasn't about increased profitability,' he says; 'the entire drive has been about improved service and sustainability in the long term.' Dr Morrow argues that for too long, general practice has languished as a passive recipient of diktats from the Department of Health and highly specialized advice coming out of hospitals, whereas it was the GPs in the community who were the right people with the right connections to deliver what was needed for the health and well-being of their local populations. What's more, sustainable primary healthcare could in turn lead to a sustainable NHS. 'We better start believing that,' he says.

The uncomfortable truth is that general practice is in a chronic state of ill health across the United Kingdom, and in some cases teetering on the edge of collapse. A combination of undermining factors has resulted in a national shortage of GPs. Against an ambition set in 2016 to increase GP numbers by 5,000 (and, more recently, the Government commitment of 6,000 more GPs by 2024/25), numbers of full-time, fully qualified GPs have actually fallen by 1,800 – a decline of 6 per cent.[1] One of the consequences has been closures in GP practices: in February 2020, there were 6,813 GP practices in England, 180 fewer than the year before – that's an average of three practice closures a week.[2] In Cambridgeshire and Peterborough, one in five general practices are what Dr Morrow calls 'financial zombies', where the GP partners, who own and run the practices and carry the risk, pay themselves less than the new recruits they employ to deliver the service. 'That's financially unsustainable,' says Dr Morrow. 'A few miles down the road there is a practice unable to recruit GPs, open only three days a week. And in some parts of the country it's not a question of how long it takes to get an appointment with your GP but rather whether or not there is a GP at all; A&E is the only accessible service. This is more costly for the healthcare system, but also means fragmented care and iatrogenic harm from having highly specialized services attempting to deliver the broad generality of medicine.' And with an aging population, ever-higher expectations and medical inflation running well ahead of growth in GDP, very little is likely to get better soon without action.

'The worst possible thing to do is go passive,' argues Dr Morrow. A keen sailor, he draws inspiration from salty dogs that have survived the most challenging of seas and relates their experience back to his general practice. 'All evidence suggests that active management is far better than being passive, irrespective of what decision you make. In difficult situations, being passive is the wrong message for the team and the wrong message for progress.'

'Change is inevitable,' he argues. 'I say to people that they may like it as it is, or prefer it as it has been, but neither of these are reasonable options for the future. The choice we have isn't between the status quo and some future state, but between two future states that we are heading toward; we can influence and shape what the future looks like.'

Two things are striking when talking to Dr Morrow. The first is an honest and totally non-judgemental assessment of reality, and the second is an eagerness to learn from across different sectors. 'We must stop saying medicine is sacrosanct,' he says, 'and adopt standardization and rigour from other disciplines. We need to think about how we keep the humanity, the trust and the relationships, but improve productivity by taking waste out of the system, because demand is only going to rise and the budget hasn't.'

Dr Morrow was a newly appointed GP at a traditional practice with six partners in Cambridgeshire when he first started talking about his vision for the future. 'I had been thinking about it for a while but hadn't acquired the vocabulary or framework to communicate it properly before then,' he says.

Dr Morrow was a medical undergraduate at Cambridge, studied clinical medicine at Oxford, and somewhere along the way picked up a first class Law degree through the Open University as well. Yet interestingly he claims that 'the most formative, stimulating educational events of my life have been run through the 21st Century Trust'. This was a charitable organization that specialized in bringing together future leaders from different professions and locations to think creatively about the key challenges facing the world. It subsequently merged with the Salzburg Global Seminar, a non-profit organization with similar objectives, founded in 1947 as a 'Marshall Plan for the mind' to challenge current and future leaders to shape a better world after the Second World War.

It was the 21st Century Trust that stimulated Dr Morrow's interest in thinking about systems and how they operated. Then a meeting at the Salzburg Global Seminar some years later on preparing for an aging population – attended by top policymakers in health systems around the world – gave Dr Morrow the intellectual framework to return to his practice with a determination to view it as a part of a bigger picture. Rather than maintaining an insular viewpoint, he wanted to look at external factors influencing the practice – technology, resources, an aging population and changing demographics of the workforce – and do some scenario building with a view to defining possible futures for the practice.

Concluding quickly that muddling along without change was unsustainable, the GPs decided that there were three possible futures for the practice: to become a niche practice, for example by serving a distinct population such as the homeless or drug addicts; to get big; or to get out. They opted for getting bigger, surmising it a necessary strategy to be able to influence both the local environment and the broader health environment, and also to accommodate changing dynamics in the workforce.

Granta Medical Practices grew to the size it is today by merging four smaller practices with similar values and aspirations. Dr Morrow's practice was at Sawston, just south of Cambridge, and it was at the school gates picking up his kids that he first struck conversation with Dr Laurence Kemp of the Linton practice down the road.

'It was apparent we had similar experiences and challenges,' said Dr Kemp. 'The more we talked about it, the more obvious it became that the solution was to come together. It took a little while to convince people,' he continued. 'I was floating ideas that might have seemed radical and some people reacted against this, but I just kept coming back to it, emphasizing the positives, and by the time we came around to formally voting on it a year or so on, it was a foregone conclusion.'

'It's been the same across all the practices that merged,' adds Dr Morrow. 'It's about building a convincing narrative and telling the story frequently enough that people begin to believe and understand it. During the merger process, we had structures in place to reassure, encourage and nurture mutual trust, and our management board gradually grew to represent the constituent practices who each felt they had a say in the system.'

How Granta Medical Practices succeeds today (having a good culture)

The four practices merged finances, lists, contracts, systems and buildings, and today patients are free to visit whichever building they prefer or that happens to be convenient on the day. Inevitably there were legal and accountancy costs to incur, and as an indication of their commitment to the new, larger practice, the partners chose to meet these costs themselves. And one of the first new appointments they made was a professional change manager: somebody from outside healthcare with a background in both the public and private sector who could manage the practice and importantly help implement the change that would shape their future. Gerard Newnham, an MBA, was appointed and remains with the practice today.

'As a leadership team, we are very clear that we need clarity of purpose, so that we understand what we are trying to achieve,' says Morrow. 'But we have worked hard on culture as well. It's a trite statement that "culture eats strategy for breakfast". Our view is that you need both, that one is the steering wheel and the other is the accelerator; you need a sense of the direction, but you also need culture to move in that direction. Matching the two together is important.' He continues, 'We're uncompromising about the central core values that we share around respect and the desire to deliver and engineer the best possible service in healthcare. Our test? "Is this the service that we would want for ourselves and our families?" If it isn't, let's fix it.'

'The maintenance of the relationship is absolutely key in terms of how we make rational decisions,' he says. 'The world of medicine is still largely an art supported by science rather than science backed up by art. One of the reasons general practice has worked in the UK is that historically it has been based on mutual respect between clinician and patient. There is trust that the clinician will do what's right for the patient to the best of his or her ability, and that the patient will engage and take the advice and understand that there is a desire to do good at the heart of the relationship. Trust and mutual respect. That's the key. If that respect breaks down and we drop back to a formulaic, protocol-driven, algorithm-led service, then trust diminishes and I think the tolerance of uncertainty, or willingness to accept opinion over fact, also diminishes.'

Listening to Dr Morrow, it's difficult not to wonder how such a healthcare service might be sustained in a time where, arguably, trust has been eroded at virtually every level of society. He responds: 'People like Ipsos MORI have done research on this. Ask people in abstract terms and they say, "Yes, I have less trust in the health service than I used to have." But if you bring it back to the specific and ask about their own doctor, then generally they say, "my doctor is great". So there is a cognitive dissonance between what people think is happening externally and their own personal experience.'

'We have a free at the point of delivery, universal health service available to everyone irrespective of their means or their ability or their background,' he says. 'That's a very unifying social construct. This morning I saw somebody who is an Oscar nominee and also somebody who is illiterate. I saw them in the same clinic, for the same length of time, with the same amount of respect for them both.' He adds matter-of-factly. 'Here, we don't believe we could provide a better service to anyone who was paying for it than we are able to provide through the National Health Service.'

Similarly, the relationships between the practice staff are about trust and mutual respect. 'We are a very non-hierarchical organization,' says Morrow. 'As chief exec, I sit and have lunch in the coffee room with our receptionists and our dispensers and our cleaner. We are all on first name terms. There's something about the ability to have the informal discussions that allows tensions to be vented and aired, issues to be understood and potentially resolved. We know quite a lot about each other and each other's lives.'

It is in large part this culture, together with an attractive working environment and a sustainable work pattern (rather than the pay, which isn't above the normal market rate) that has resulted in young GPs being handed a waiting list if they apply to work at Granta, while other practices struggle to recruit. When the decision was first made to 'get bigger', one of the first challenges that was identified was the changing demographics of the workforce. Pointing to a current trend, Dr Morrow says, 'I spoke to 75 local GP trainees recently, and the majority of them want to work no more than three days a week. Some are choosing portfolio careers where they do two or three days in general practice and maybe a day of research or a day working in a hospice. But quite a few are saying they'd like time to look after their garden, or their children. These are people in their mid-20s, deciding that if they're going to be working until they're 70 before they get a pension, which is what they're being told, they had better work in a sustainable, balanced way.'

This is very different from when Dr Morrow entered the profession. 'I don't suppose I would have been accepted on anything less than full-time,' he says. Arguably it's a privilege to have the choice. But Morrow doesn't dwell on this. It's a fact. Something he can't change, so he works with it. A good number of Granta GPs work three days a week; one works just one day a week.

'Historically the Holy Grail of general practice has been continuity,' he says. 'Seeing the same doctor who knows you and your family every time. There is some recent research saying that continuity reduces your risk of death, but we also recognize that absolute continuity with one individual is impossible given the demands and demographics of the workforce, as well as that of the population.'

At Granta, they spend a lot of time asking patients (or practice members, as they prefer to call them) what they want. 'When we talked about continuity being the Holy Grail of general practice, it seemed that actually it was the doctors who rated it far more highly than the practice members. For many, the phrase that kept being trotted out was, "I don't mind which of you I see, you are all very good, I just need to see someone quickly when I need it."'

'If a practice member rings and say it's urgent, we guarantee we will see them that day,' says Dr Morrow. The mean time between a practice member contacting Granta and getting an appointment is two hours, and quite often an appointment is offered within minutes. Using best judgement is important. If a receptionist has concerns about somebody on the telephone and judges the situation urgent enough to interrupt a doctor in surgery, that's not a problem. The doctors will listen.

Strategy for improved flow and productivity

So at Granta Medical Practices, all the staff members are very clear about the practice's culture: that it is rooted in mutual trust and respect, and that the patient's interests are at the heart of every decision made. Is it good enough for my family? If not, fix it. They are also pragmatic about the changing demographics of the workforce, adapting so that staff can work part-time. And the final part of the equation they have focused on is a well-considered strategy to improve productivity by taking waste out of the system, 'because,' says Morrow, 'demand is close to insatiable, it is only going to rise, and the budget won't'.

'We have simply brought some basic business school 101 operational stuff into medicine,' says Morrow. 'It's viewed as anathema for many doctors who think that medicine is different from every other industry or profession. It isn't. There are some core principles such as segmentation and streaming that improve flow and productivity.'

At Granta Medical Practices, they have segmented their service into five areas, which are striking in their common sense:

1) Urgent care: For 90 per cent of patients, speed of access was rated more important than individual continuity. Granta has a rapid access clinic and operates telephone triage.

2) Planned care: Routine general practice where practice members can book consultations with a clinician of their choice up to six weeks in advance. The practice is open for extended hours five days a week.

3) Frail elderly: The ability to care for those who are housebound or terminally ill is a key part of looking after the more vulnerable in society. 'It used to be the case that home visits got shoe-horned into the middle of the day, after morning surgery,' says Morrow, 'which meant that if a patient had to go into hospital for tests it was late afternoon or evening before they did so, and they often ended up staying overnight. We know this is the worst possible thing we can do to a frail elderly person because they can lose a third of their muscle mass in just a few days; if they weren't dependent when they went in, they will be dependent within several days of admission. Even if nothing is done to you, going into hospital is a health hazard.' By joining forces, Granta's practices immediately achieved scale to make it financially viable to employ paramedics. Today Granta employs three paramedics who form a visiting team for the frail elderly in their homes from 8 o'clock in the morning, so if a hospital visit is required, they are there and back and settled in their own homes the same day. Having a dedicated visiting team allows the

paramedics to build a relationship with the elderly in their homes; it offers continuity at a time when a patient most needs it, and with real-time technology, there can always be a doctor at hand to support a visit if necessary.

4) Long-term conditions: Granta has also redesigned the care of patients with chronic conditions who require regular reviews and monitoring. Historically reviews were organized around specific diseases – hypertension, or diabetes, or thyroid – but the reality is that many people live with multiple conditions, not just one, and as such were obliged to attend multiple clinics, wasting their time as well as the doctors' time. This has been totally turned on its head so that now the reviews for chronic conditions are patient-centred, not disease-centred. The reviews are also largely carried out by the administrative team, with a patient only being invited to see a doctor if required. This saves a lot of time. If a patient only requires a tweak in the dosage of their medication, for example, he or she can be informed by letter, text or phone, or a five-minute face-to-face appointment, which allows the team to carve out longer 45-minute appointments where they are most needed.

5) Specialist clinics: Granta currently has vasectomy, ear micro-suction and minor surgery clinics, with plans for hand, ENT, paediatrics and ophthalmology clinics.

'We are incredibly proud of what we do here,' says Morrow. 'We have had no extra resourcing; we're on the same national contract as every other general practice in the country, but by re-engineering our systems we have demonstrated positive deviance in output by taking waste out of the system. Our nurses know exactly how much the dressings cost, and we're very conscious about not over-prescribing antibiotics. We are in the bottom quartile of antibiotic prescribers in the country, which is a measure of health and well-being; and we are one of the best practices in the country in terms of low admission rates for respiratory disease. Amongst the practices in the area we do better on many measures, and we think this is because of the structure that we have: accessibility when people want it, and intelligent, programmed reviews for chronic conditions.'

Granta Medical Practices is now at about the size it wants to be. 'Around 45,000 patients makes sense for us,' says Morrow. 'We have 126 people on the core clinical team and aim to have no more than 150, the size you can grow to comfortably before fragmenting into silos. A bit like a regiment, there is a size of unit which works well, where there's a loyalty and people look out for each other.'

Plans for the future

But this doesn't mean they don't have ambitions for the future. Granta has recently restructured its traditional board of GP partners into a tighter executive team to mirror that of a normal company board, with Dr Morrow as chief executive, Stefan Scholtes, professor of health management from Cambridge Judge Business School, as non-executive chair, Gerard Newnham as practice change manager, and two of the GPs as clinical and medical directors, plus a board secretary. 'It was a unanimous decision,' says Morrow. The partners who ceded operational control did so voluntarily and continue to be shareholders, but have delegated decision-making to the executive board essentially to speed up the process and deliver the best possible healthcare.

If there can be any criticism of Granta Medical Practices, it might be that the staff have been so focused on 'getting bigger' and implementing their strategy that they could be regarded as somewhat isolationist, building their own future without much regards for the Clinical Commissioning Group or NHS England. 'We've been rather remote and self-reliant,' Morrow admits, 'but now we are working hard to build and improve relationships.'

In a theme that runs through the execution of strategy in every sector, communicating to the greater world is critical to win the support of others and for growth. 'Now, if the local radio or television station ring up and want a doctor's opinion, we say yes.' While recognizing a number of the staff still exhibit a nervousness around the media, he says, 'an engagement with the local, regional population is important. It gives us credibility. And it gives our practice members – and those in the organization – an enormous pride that we are the "go to" place for an opinion.'

They have also worked hard at building relationships with the broader health system. Morrow is in regular contact with the chief executive of Addenbrooke's hospital in Cambridge, as well as the county council. He also has a WhatsApp group going with the local MP and other chief execs, 'so, if you like, we are at the top table of how we design and co-ordinate things. Our model here is now being used as the shorthand by the hospital for how they view the future of general practice. They would like six "Grantas" – units of this sort of size – so they can work collaboratively with them, rather than the 100 or so regional practices as there are now.'

'It is a marker of our aspiration that we want to be in the community, and of the community, and create a structure which is fit for the next 50 to 70 years of the National Health Service. A structure which is set up in a way that it is not going to be privatized and become part of a multinational conglomerate,' says Morrow. 'We have photographs on the wall of the doctors here that date back to 1842 in continuity, and we want to make sure that the people who work here continue to have mutual respect and shared ownership of the organization, and still deliver a service for our local population.'

The question is can this model, developed and implemented so successfully by Granta Medical Practices, influence a broader system? They think it can. 'There is nothing that we are doing which is magic,' says Morrow. 'It's about a culture and an ethos and a vision. But we think we have developed a model with some merits which others may wish to copy, or which we can help them adapt for local circumstances.'

In an exciting development, Granta is working on a project to set up a Primary Care Innovation Academy at the Judge Business School at Cambridge University, to apply business and academic analysis and rigour to what they have been doing, and to offer an executive programme for other GPs and managers, as a way of disseminating some of the lessons learned. Despite COVID-19, an inaugural cohort was run in 2020 that brought together the Clinical Directors from the emerging Primary Care Networks of General Practices, both from within the Cambridgeshire and Peterborough system and further afield. And in parallel, Granta is progressing on its own journey as well. 'If we can pull it off, our idea is to create an Employee Ownership Trust – a model also used by the UK department store John Lewis – where we create a single team around our practice population; this includes our occupational therapists and physiotherapists, specialists from the hospital, as well as people from the county council and social services.' But there is an acknowledgement that this transformation can't be taken without a cash injection, and as such Morrow is in conversation with the Department of Health, promoting the idea as something that could be replicated across the country.

Few are in doubt that there is a need for some form of systemic change in the organization of primary healthcare and the NHS. There is hope that such transformation might be welcomed universally. Meanwhile, while the system continues in a sub-optimal state of organization, there is within it an explosion of medical science and technology that will change the face of medical care as we know it. 'Personalized medicine is the future,' says Morrow. 'Just recently we had a patient with cancer whose tumour tissue was sent off to the lab to be typed; we know everything about the genetics of the cancer, including which drugs are likely to work and which are not, and that's shaping his treatment, which is amazing.'

'But ultimately,' he adds, 'when we look to the future and how technology might shape it, and ask (inevitably) if we might be cared for by robots, the answer is in the words of a Silicon Valley entrepreneur: "We who are mortal will always want to be cared for by those who understand mortality."' Morrow describes how recently he visited a patient who was within perhaps 48 hours of his death at home. 'Will you do me a favour?' the patient asked. 'You looked after my wife so well when she died here in this bed, will you do the same for me?' Morrow answered that of course he would and asked him how he was coping, and the man pointed to his CD player, 'The best technical medicine you could have, Handel's *Messiah*, but more importantly doctor, how are *you* coping?' Morrow told him that it was a privilege to look after him at the end of his life, but that he saw pregnant mums and new babies too, the full spectrum. And the man said, 'You see new life into the world and old life like mine out of the world to make space, it must be very satisfying.'

'This is the bit that technology can never replace,' says Morrow, 'and it's why we need real people and why we need relationships and trust.'

References

1. Nuffield Trust, 'The NHS workforce in numbers'
2. https://www.bma.org.uk/advice-and-support/nhs-delivery-and-workforce/pressures/pressures-in-general-practice

CHAPTER TWO

Executing Strategy on Behalf of the United Nations

We can choose to deal with inhumane situations in a humane way, we can turn the world around and create positive lessons for ourselves and others.

Zlata Filipović, Bosnian–Irish diarist, who lived in Sarajevo as a child during the Bosnian war

This story exemplifies courage, commitment and an utter conviction to get a job done, to make the lives of ordinary people better and in doing so to save two million people from starvation. It is about defining a strategy and implementing it.

Businessmen and women are frequently required to navigate an uncomfortably complex and opaque environment, more so today than ever before. But few things are quite as complex as the fog of war, and in particular a three-sided civil war, where nothing is as it appears.

In January 1994, when Lieutenant-General Sir Michael Rose took on the role of Commander of the United Nations Protection Force in Bosnia and Herzegovina, its peacekeeping mission was on the point of collapse. The city of Sarajevo had been reduced to a rubble of shattered buildings. It was a city under siege in which its 350,000 inhabitants lived like rats in cellars, venturing out only at night to search for means of survival. For near-on two years, there had been no electricity or running water, and no adequate supplies of food or fuel. Each day, the people of Sarajevo faced the constant threat of being killed or maimed by some 1,200 shells that fell on the city, or by the seldom seen but ever-watchful snipers. Since the start of the war it was estimated by the Bosnian government that 10,000 people had been killed in Sarajevo, 3,000 of them children. It was a city of hatred, deprivation and death; a grim symbol of the savagery of man and the fragility of civilization.

Sir Michael Rose's primary task was a humanitarian one: to protect and provide aid, as far as that were possible, for civilians caught in the crossfire, irrespective of which side of the conflict they were on. This might seem like a straightforward, easily understood goal – however it was anything but that. In a civil war, there is no such thing as neutrality or an impartial peacekeeper. Humanitarian aid becomes a strategic factor that the warring parties seek to exploit to their own advantage. And the differing agendas and points of view didn't stop at the geographical boundary of a once-united country disintegrated into civil war. The international community was also at odds. On the one hand, America and the Muslim states demanded that the UN mission be used to pursue war-fighting goals, while on the other hand, Russia and Greece wanted a more conciliatory attitude toward the Serbs. In the middle, trying to balance the debate, stood Britain and France. It happened that these two countries had the largest number of troops on the ground. The position of Germany was somewhere between France and America, but its influence was limited because of its history in the two world wars in Yugoslavia. Importantly, none of the Troop Contributing Nations wished to see their peacekeepers drawn into warfighting for which they were neither equipped nor mandated to do.

As a soldier, Sir Michael Rose understood how important it was to operate from a firm political base, and to keep the politicians behind what he was trying to do. But with 185 nations represented by the UN, this clearly wasn't going to be easy. Rose's immediate predecessor, Belgian Lieutenant-General Francis Briquemont, had unexpectedly resigned in disgust six months early, claiming a 'fantastic' gap between the constant and conflicting demands imposed by the UN Security Council resolutions and the support he was getting both politically and materially. He also said he could no longer withstand the psychological pressures of the job. The Bosnian government had just declared it was ready to move on to an all-out offensive and, in response, the Bosnian Serbs had mobilized their entire population for war. At the same time, the UN High Commissioner for Refugees, Sadako Ogata, had reported that the quantity of aid being delivered had fallen to a dangerously low level because of renewed outbreaks of fighting and the continual hijacking of aid convoys. The US–British relationship was under severe strain as a result of the radically opposed policies being pursued over Bosnia, and the cooling of relationships between the US and Russia risked bringing about a return of the Cold War. NATO was concerned about its own credibility, and serious differences were emerging within the organization about its future role now that the Cold War had ended.

Meanwhile, in Bosnia, a mortar bomb had killed six small children as they tobogganed down a slope on the outskirts of Sarajevo, and the morale in the United Nations Protection Force (UNPROFOR) was at an all-time low. No surprise that General Philippe Morillon, who had preceded Briquemont as UNPROFOR Commander in Bosnia, had called the operation 'mission impossible'.

Deciding to take on the job/initial steps

When Rose was approached by the Military Secretary to find out how he might react should his name be put forward to replace Briquemont as Commander of UNPROFOR in Bosnia, he responded without hesitation that he would accept the job should it be offered to him. Considering the post was universally regarded as something of a poisoned chalice, this certainty on his part would have been welcomed. As with any complex situation, leadership commitment to the cause is an essential starting point.

Rose was also very well qualified for the job. A military man through and through, he was Oxford-educated, followed by six months at the Sorbonne where he picked up fluent French before being commissioned into the Coldstream Guards. Rose then joined the Special Air Service (SAS) – an elite Special Forces regiment in which initiative, unorthodox intelligence, ruthlessness and cold courage are highly regarded. It was in the SAS that Rose made his reputation: first as the man in charge of the SAS unit that stormed the Iranian embassy in May 1980 – never to be forgotten by those of us watching primetime television on a bank holiday Monday when both the BBC and ITV interrupted their scheduled programming to broadcast live footage of flash bangs and men in black abseiling off the embassy rooftop – and then in the Falklands War, where his negotiating of the final surrender of the Argentine forces undoubtedly helped prevent the war from spreading into Port Stanley.

Rose spent his last year before taking on the role of Commander of UNPROFOR as the Deputy Joint Force Commander overseeing the UK contribution to the UN mission in the former Yugoslavia, and he had visited Bosnia on several occasions. He had also been Commandant at the Staff College in Camberley shortly after the end of the Cold War, where he had begun to look in some detail at peacekeeping operations in support of the UN. A year in Bosnia would give him opportunity to put many of his emergent ideas into practice.

Rose wasted no time and threw himself into his new role. He understood that no matter the organization or setting, there are some obstacles to success that remain the same. Trained in military history, he was all too familiar with the Prussian General Carl von Clausewitz's identification of two ever-present factors that are often overlooked: fog and friction. Rose knew that he would be exchanging the relatively sane, routine existence of a senior British army officer for life in a brutal, chaotic environment where the corrosive effects of continuous war had destroyed all notions of justice, and where deceit and treachery had become a way of life. But he also knew that he was taking on a mission that, having been shaped and evolved in the fog of war, was enshrouded in fog itself. He needed to simplify the mission. And he desperately needed to iron out the friction between the opposing factions within the United Nations. The multiple nations represented in the UN had different priorities, different views and different goals, but he had to find common ground and have them singing with a single voice.

First job: simplify the muddled mission objectives. When Rose took over, the UN Security Council had passed at least 17 different resolutions in response to each humanitarian crisis in Bosnia that had inevitably occurred in the fast deteriorating situation. The problem was that the resolutions started to counter one another, and it was manifestly impossible to pursue them all, hence the intolerable psychological pressure experienced by Rose's predecessor. With great clarity and confidence that comes from experience and station, Rose took a metaphorical red pen and drew a line through all the resolutions, and started again.

His view was that the replacement mission should comprise the following three main elements, in order of priority:

1) The delivery of humanitarian aid on which so many people's lives depended.
2) The creation of conditions for a political settlement of the war.
3) Preventing the conflict from spreading beyond Bosnia.

By adopting a more robust approach in the UN dealings with the local warlords who had so paralysed the mission, and by more closely integrating the activities of the humanitarian agencies involved in Bosnia, he also hoped to improve the flow of aid. Above all, he was determined to confront the negative propaganda surrounding UNPROFOR that was damaging the image of the mission in the eyes of the world.

He took these ideas to the army Staff College, and with half a dozen colleagues he 'red teamed' the strategy, testing and challenging its effectiveness by assuming an adversarial point of view until he was convinced of the strategy and its scope. As in business and in life, it's often tempting to assume one can do more, but Rose was very clear on this point. There was to be no mission creep. 'A clear mission allows the structure to be put in place to execute that mission,' he says. 'Everybody understands the mission; it's achievable, and measurable.'

The next job was to convince his colleagues in the United Nations and get them on side. Travelling with his new military assistant, Lieutenant-Colonel Simon Shadbolt, he spent a busy week visiting the capital cities of the key international players involved in Bosnia. First port of call was Paris, to visit the French Chief of Defence Staff Admiral Jacques Lanxade and his team. The French were the largest contributors to the mission in Bosnia and their support would be key to Rose's ability to implement a new approach.

No doubt a face-to-face meeting was essential for Rose to clearly explain his strategy and hopefully win approval, but it did no harm as well that Rose was able to communicate fluently in French. His time at the Sorbonne was coming into its own. Rose's love of the French language, and France in general, succeeded in defusing the considerable suspicions the French were harbouring about the arrival of a British commander in what – up until then – had been a French-dominated mission. Admiral Lanxade strongly supported Rose's plan, and was particularly delighted by his intention to be tougher on the warring parties. A close working relationship between the two most important players on the ground in Bosnia was securely sealed.

The next day, Rose was back in England for an interview at Downing Street with the Prime Minister, John Major. Armed with the latest thinking from Paris, they were able to discuss the different courses of action facing Britain's military, which ranged from pulling out the troops to reluctantly being dragged into a war. There was discussion about a greater use of air power – a subject that was going to repeatedly raise its head in the course of the following year – and Rose suggested that although NATO air power certainly had an important role to play, it couldn't be applied much above a tactical level without collapsing the entire peacekeeping mission. Rose left the meeting with the impression that John Major fervently believed in the humanitarian role being played by the UN in Bosnia, and that Britain had a special contribution to make; he was not about to pull out the troops. John Major's commitment to the cause allowed Rose to develop many initiatives that otherwise would have been impossible, and despite the many pressures that Major subsequently came under from his own government and from his allies in 1994, he never altered the peacekeeping basis upon which British troops were deployed.

The following day, Rose and Simon Shadbolt were on a transatlantic flight to New York for important discussions with the UN and the ambassadors of the different countries involved in Bosnia. This was going to be a critical meeting to ensure countries with very different agendas were aligned.

It was here for the first time that Rose met Kofi Annan, then the head of the UN peacekeeping department, together with one of his closest advisers, Shashi Tharoor. It left Rose in an optimistic mood. Any preconceptions Rose may have had about the poor quality of UN bureaucrats were instantly dispersed as he found himself talking to two individuals with remarkably detailed knowledge of the Balkans. Rose was impressed by their grasp of the military technicalities involved in maintaining a peacekeeping operation in such difficult circumstances, by their political acumen, and by their seemingly inexhaustible energy. He was left feeling confident that whatever problems might arise in Bosnia, they would be dealt with in a rational and helpful manner by the UN headquarters in New York.

Now it was time to present his ideas to the UN officials. With clarity and confidence, Rose explained the need for a proper campaign plan and a more coherent approach, and expressed his firm belief that much could be achieved by the UN in Bosnia if the political, military and humanitarian aid effort could be better co-ordinated. He also left no doubt as to where his loyalties lay. He told them that during his tenure as commander in Bosnia, he would never publicly disagree on matters of policy with the UN or criticize them personally, explaining that he came from a tradition where the military were wholly subordinate to the political body, and that to rehearse any disagreements they might have in front of the media would be inimical to the mission and damage the UN's credibility.

Finally, he shared with them the belief that a more robust military approach to the peacekeeping mission would be required if it were to survive, and presented them with the outline of the campaign plan that identified the aid delivery programme as the highest priority of the mission. It was agreed that the secondary task, which was the creation of conditions necessary for peaceful resolution of the conflict, could only be accomplished in the right political context and that military forces alone could not deliver political solutions.

Sir David Hannay, the UK Permanent Representative to the UN, reminded Rose of the various hazards and pitfalls awaiting him in Bosnia, not least of which was the media. Rose was all too aware that reports of failure would only undermine the resolve of the troop-contributing nations to continue with their mission.

Another important point of discussion was the size of the UN headquarters in Bosnia, which in Rose's view had grown to grotesque proportions, 'more like a holiday camp than a military command cell'. And indeed, the headquarters were situated in a ski hotel in Kiseljak in the Fojnica Valley, built in 1984 for the winter Olympics. They accommodated some 500 UN personnel, and the hotel bar was always full.

Rose felt the headquarters needed to be drastically reduced in size, but in suggesting this to Kofi Annan he was met with resistance. Kofi Annan agreed with him in principle, but explained that this would be politically delicate. Troop-contributing nations had come to regard the seniority and rank of their staff in the HQ as something of a status symbol; it was comfortable, a good distance from the fighting around Sarajevo, and the place of choice for the majority of the senior contingent commanders. There was also the matter of the national 'red card' held by the commanders, which allowed them to overrule any decision Rose might make if it was considered to be against their national interests. This offered their constituents at home some reassurance about how their peacekeeping troops would be used – particularly important after recent experiences in Somalia, where the general view was that the US element of the mission had hijacked the command chain, which had resulted in unnecessary UN casualties. Kofi Annan expressed the view that it would be almost impossible to reduce the size of the national staffs in the headquarters for these reasons. It had been tried before, and failed.

These discussions were followed by a civilized lunch at the very elegant apartment of Sir David Hannay, overlooking the East River in New York. All the main players involved in Bosnia were present. Toward the end of the lunch, Rose was invited to describe his campaign plan for Bosnia, which he did, finishing by asking everyone around the table for their support for the new strategy he had outlined. It was with some relief for the majority that a clear plan was on offer to cut through the confused political environment as it stood, and Kofi Annan immediately responded with a strong statement committing the UN to supporting Rose's ideas, leaving little room for debate among the others.

On the face of things, it would appear that the main players involved in Bosnia, despite varying and different agendas of their own, had found common ground on which they could agree. Rose had successfully achieved his primary mission of creating a coalition to achieve a common goal. But there was an undercurrent of tension that would repeatedly swell up and finally surface. The US Ambassador to the United Nations, Madeleine Albright, asked Rose what value he placed on air strikes. Rose explained that in his view there was no case for mounting a strategic air campaign in Bosnia similar to the one in the Gulf War; the circumstances were entirely different. However, he had no problem with the use of close air support in self-defence or to support the overall peacekeeping strategy, provided that the use of force was proportionate, timely and sufficiently precise. It was a message that Rose would find himself peddling repeatedly throughout his time in Bosnia.

Landing in Sarajevo

A few days later, Rose was sitting in the cargo hold of a giant Ilyushin Il-76 UN plane, destination Sarajevo. After a brief change-in-command ceremony with the exhausted Lieutenant-General Francis Briquemont, Rose was driven from the airport into Sarajevo itself, sweeping through the main Serb roadblock, Sierra Four, without stopping. A year before, a Bosnian government minister had been killed here, sitting in the back of a French armoured personnel carrier. They drove past wrecked tanks and shattered buildings, incongruent in a modern city, but something that was going to become all too familiar to Rose over the next 12 months.

As they crossed the conflict line on to the Bosnian side, a detachment of 120mm mortars opened fire close to the road to their left. Bosnian forces were shelling Serb positions on the hills above the city. Rose asked rather nervously what was happening and Viktor Andreev, the Russian UN civil adviser in Sarajevo, who had come to greet Rose, told him there was nothing to worry about. In the eyes of the Bosnian government, there was no such thing as a purely military action, he explained – only political action. They always greeted new arrivals to Sarajevo in this way, and the Serbs always responded in kind with artillery fire on the city. Thus visitors were given a practical demonstration of the aggression being committed against the State of Bosnia. In this way, the Bosnian government hoped to persuade the West to become involved in the war on their side. When Rose asked about the civilian casualties that resulted from this tactic, Viktor Andreev shrugged and replied that civilians mattered less to the Bosnian government than images of suffering and war. Rose spoke about this tactic to Madeleine Albright; she confirmed that the US Administration knew what was happening, but there was very little they could do about it.

The location of the UNPROFOR quarters in Sarajevo was a large rambling building in the centre of town known as the 'Residency'. Built in the distinctive style of the Austro-Hungarian Empire, it was, in Tito's time, the Delegates Club, where senior officials of the Yugoslav Communist Party came each day to eat their lunch. The building had been extensively bugged by Tito's secret police, and Rose had been warned that the bugging continued, this time by the Bosnian government's security service, eager to keep track of the UN's deliberations. The Residency stood in its own grounds beside the US embassy, and was to be Rose's home for a year.

Though chaos ruled throughout the city – electricity, water and even food were intermittent and there was the constant threat of danger – the Residency maintained a sense of order as far as circumstances would allow. An operating rhythm was established and a military discipline prevailed. Before Rose even arrived, his team from Britain had set to work and completely reorganized the layout, increasing office space at the expense of accommodation.

Colour Sergeant 'Percy' Pearce of the Coldstream Guards went one step further and gathered together all the staff of the Residency, most of whom had been working in the building since the days of the Delegates Club, and explained to them that despite the fact they were being paid by the Bosnian government, he was now their boss. Things were going to be very different now they were to be done the Coldstream way. Accounts would be properly run, the pilfering of food would stop, and rats and rubbish would no longer be permitted on the premises. He established a fair system of duty rosters and rewards, and in no time the morale of the staff had risen greatly and the Residency was run like St James's Palace. Another member of the team was so appalled by the squalid state of the Residency when they moved in that he ruthlessly helped reorganize the whole establishment, and as a symbol of his refusal to let civilized standards slip he changed his socks every day and went for a run in defiance of the shells and snipers who made life so difficult for everybody in Sarajevo.

Courage is a theme that shouts loud when hearing the story of peacekeeping in Bosnia. Rose typically points to the heroism of the soldiers who came in their thousands, wearing the distinctive blue beret and uniform of the United Nations, as well as the men and women who came from all corners of the world to help work for peace, many of whom were volunteer reservists. These peacekeepers aimed to alleviate the suffering of all the peoples of the Balkans, and to try through peaceful means to bring about an end to the war. More than 300 of them didn't return home.

There was moral and physical courage in the leadership as well. Rose made a decision very early on to walk the streets of Sarajevo, much to the surprise of many of the citizens with whom he stopped to speak, who were accustomed to seeing UN peacekeepers driving by at high speed in armoured cars and who never saw their own political leaders on the street. For Rose, it was important to spend time walking about the city, to identify as closely as possible with its people and to stave off any danger of succumbing to the siege mentality that he had observed among a few of the peacekeepers. For the same reason, he made a conscious decision not to wear a flak jacket or helmet; he felt it created a psychological barrier when talking to people who didn't have such protection. There is many a fine photo of Rose in shirtsleeves and beret, with visiting politicians looking decidedly overdressed in full armour cladding beside him – a strong visual message if ever there was one.

It was on one such walk through the city that Rose saw a sniper carrying a Simonov rifle leave his position in a ruined block of flats. He was a good-looking boy, blond with blue eyes, in his late teens. But when he looked at Rose, his eyes were as dead as the bodies that littered the Sarajevo streets. It wasn't Rose's war, but as a human being he was involved, and he came to understand that this sniper represented as great a threat to civilization itself as he did to the citizens of Sarajevo. It took a long while, but peacekeepers finally came to the aid of the people of Sarajevo and Bosnia. This was Rose's mission.

Closing the headquarters in Kiseljak

By the end of his first week in Bosnia it was plain to Rose that the peacekeeping mission lacked forward strategy or central direction, as he had long suspected. It had become unstructured and fragmented, and the UN command organization itself was unwieldy. While Rose, as UN Commander, was stationed in the UNPROFOR quarters in Sarajevo, the UN Chief of Staff was in the main UN headquarters in the former Olympic village of Kiseljak, some 20 miles away on the other side of the conflict line. The communications between the two sites left a lot to be desired. As a result, Rose discovered he and his Chief of Staff were out of touch for much of the time, and (as had been the case with the previous UN Commander, Briquemont) the staff at the Residency just had to get on with what they thought was the best course of action, with little central organization and direction of activity.

It was the headquarters in Kiseljak that directly commanded all units and controlled all operations that took place in Bosnia, including all military and aid convoys. But there was no intermediate or brigade level of command, except in Sarajevo where the French had unilaterally established its own sector headquarters. As a result, the UN staff worked extraordinarily long hours and had become bogged down in a web of interrelated negotiations with the three warring parties. Their collective inability to take rapid and relevant decisions in response to a fast-changing situation was beginning to undermine their morale, and indeed the credibility of the entire UN mission.

It didn't help that Kiseljak was so geographically removed from the fighting around Sarajevo. The atmosphere in the comfortable, centrally heated headquarters was inward-looking, and each department seemed to spend much of its time trying to find out what the other UN departments were doing. Somebody had mischievously suggested to Rose that the headquarters were consuming more rations than they were delivering to the people of Bosnia. Certainly it was nothing short of a tragedy that bureaucracy was thwarting the efforts of so many committed, hard-working people in the UN and that the mission was failing. The delivery of aid had fallen by 40 per cent of required levels, and the United Nations High Commission for Refugees (UNHCR) had produced a paper predicting that some 800,000 people might perish if aid targets weren't met the following winter, when temperatures could be expected to remain below freezing for many weeks.

It was time for Rose to take action and radically reduce the size of Kiseljak headquarters. Kofi Annan had told him it would be virtually impossible, and now, in Bosnia, the same message was being repeated. Rose spoke first of all with the Chief of Staff of the headquarters, a British officer with whom he'd worked previously in Northern Ireland, and whom he respected. Rose asked him to assemble the commanders of all the military units in Bosnia in the headquarters on the following Saturday, so he could issue a new set of mission orders that reflected his more robust approach to peacekeeping. He also suggested that the heads of all the aid agencies should be invited to the meeting, so they too could be involved in the new planning.

The Chief of Staff was horrified. He believed any attempt to adopt a more robust approach to peacekeeping would upset the delicate relationships that existed between the UN and the warring parties. He also strongly advised against issuing orders to the UN unit commanders, arguing that it would be better to use a process of consultation and negotiation to persuade them to accept the new strategy. It was, he said, impossible to change the culture and the structure of the UN in the way Rose intended.

Rose believed otherwise, but nonetheless asked the Chief of Staff to give him a critical path analysis of the linkages and deals that he felt would be necessary to follow if the mission was to progress. The Chief of Staff handed him a diagram that could best be described as a tangled ball of wool. Rose was sympathetic. He saw the Chief of Staff as a deeply caring and highly intelligent individual, but feared he had become a prisoner of the overly bureaucratic nature of the UN command structure.

On the next Saturday, as planned, Rose went ahead and presented his ideas at a meeting of the assembled commanding officers and representatives from UNHCR and the other NGOs working on the delivery of aid. At the same time, he told everybody that Kiseljak would be closed; electricity, central heating and hot water would be cut off, except to keep running a small logistics base. The news was received by some of the staff in dismay. It was a tough measure, but nothing like as tough as it would be for the civilians starving on the streets of Sarajevo if the mission didn't succeed in delivering aid.

Many of the staff left Bosnia for greener fields elsewhere, but those who were committed to rebuilding the humanitarian operation received the news with enthusiasm. Some 70 or so people from Kiseljak packed their bags and moved willingly to the Residency in Sarajevo, despite the obvious danger of being in the city. Rose had cabins built in the garden to accommodate the new arrivals, and numbers, which included a small NATO air-tasking cell, were kept roughly to a manageable 100.

By closing Kiseljak and moving a slimmed-down headquarters to Sarajevo, Rose was able to reorganize the Bosnia-Herzegovina Command into three separate sector commands: one in Gornji Vakuf in the south-west; another encompassing Sarajevo and eastern Bosnia, including the two Muslim enclaves of Žepa and Goražde; and the third in the north-west of Bosnia, including the Muslim enclave of Srebrenica.

To make sense of the restructuring, Rose also needed to align the work of the three sector commands with that of UNHCR (responsible for delivering aid), and the most logical way to achieve this was to site

UNPROFOR headquarters and UNHCR headquarters at each level of command in the same geographical locations across Bosnia, so that together they would be responsible for organizing all aid and military convoys in their region and could respond immediately to any urgent requests or crises. The head of the UNHCR mission to the former Yugoslavia, Nicholas Morris, welcomed this decision. The mission in Bosnia was the first time that UNHCR had been required to deliver aid in a war situation, and they had to learn as they went along. It was a huge relief for Morris to hear directly from the new UNPROFOR commander that the delivery of aid was his number one objective, and that he would defer to Morris's advice and command his troops to do everything within their power to help.

Getting aid moving again

One of those things within UNPROFOR's power was to ban any deals being struck with the local warlords to obstruct the passage of convoys, which historically had resulted in much of the aid being held up or not delivered at all. From now on, each of the three sector commanders would present a unified plan for humanitarian assistance to the political leaders of their three communities, who would then be held responsible for any blocking or hijacking of convoys by their respective armies. If aid were prevented from getting through, the UN would not hesitate to expose the illegal actions of the warlords to the press, or to explain the consequences of their actions to the people.

A case in point were two convoy routes, one running from the coast via Mostar and Konjic to Sarajevo, and the second running from the north, through Zenica and Zavidovići to Tuzla. Fighting between the three factions had closed both these routes for many months, and several bridges had been destroyed. In order to ensure there would be no more attacks on these convoy routes, Rose ordered a platoon of Danish Leopard tanks – known as Snow Leopards, because they were painted white – to move immediately from Split, where they had been languishing and doing very little, to Tuzla.

There was a degree of contention over this. Rose had been told that the use of tanks for peacekeeping duties was a politically sensitive issue and that he would need permission from Zagreb and from New York, and that this had not been forthcoming. So Rose telephoned the Danish squadron commander of the tank company and asked him directly if he could take on such a task. The commander welcomed the opportunity. He explained that his men were fed up waiting for specific orders; they had been messed about for nearly three months, having been moved from Zagreb to Belgrade and then on to Split – and he felt his own bosses in Denmark would support the mission as they too had expressed disappointment at the lack of proper employment for the unit. The tanks rolled that night while the ground was still frozen, and although there was some bureaucratic criticism from members of the Security Council about Rose's failure to consult with New York, Rose learned that the UN administration in New York secretly welcomed such independent action from the field, as long as it proved successful.

It wasn't long before Rose implemented his hardline tactics to make sure that convoys could pass through a control point known as Sierra One, on the road between Kiseljak and the besieged city of Sarajevo. This was the only usable land route along which the UN was able to deliver aid to the 350,000 people who inhabited the city – and it was controlled by the Bosnian Serbs.

For two days, Sierra One had been closed to traffic on the orders of General Manojlo Milovanović, Chief of Staff to General Ratko Mladić, so Rose issued strict instructions that all convoys with proper clearances were to force their passage through the checkpoint. These instructions were merely enforcing the Geneva agreement signed on 18 November 1993 by the leaders of all the warring parties, including President of Republika Srpska, Radovan Karadžić, to allow free passage of aid through Bosnia. But once again, Rose's Chief of Staff advised against the action, concerned the Serbs might respond by halting all aid delivery across the territory they controlled. Rose had to remind him that the UN was, as it stood, failing in its mission to allow aid through. If they didn't do something drastic to reverse the trend, all credibility would be lost.

Rose ordered his old regiment, the Coldstream Guards, to break through Sierra One, taking the precaution first to ask Captain Nick Costello (a British army officer whose family were Krajina Serbs from Knin) to explain to the Serbs manning the roadblock what was happening, in the hope this might prevent them from opening fire. On his previous tour of duty in Bosnia, Costello had got to know the Serbs well, and sure enough he knew the woman who was interpreter at the roadblock. She pleaded with him not to press ahead with the enforcement plan. The Serbs liked the British, she said, and him in particular, but they would be forced to open fire if any attempt was made to break through the barrier. She didn't want to see him die.

'Well,' said Costello, 'you have your orders and I have mine. But before you do anything stupid, take a look above. I wouldn't want to see you die either.' As he spoke, four A-10 aircraft from NATO roared overhead. Costello gave her a cheery wave and closed down the hatch of the armoured vehicle he was in, and the company moved forward through the flimsy barricade. As the Warrior vehicles drove down the road with the A-10s circling menacingly overhead, the Serb soldiers were seen dashing to their trenches and grabbing their weapons, but they held their fire.

The new instructions to take action and the consequential reduction in the stopping or hijacking of convoys, increased morale considerably and the delivery of humanitarian aid began to increase. In March 1994, from a failing situation at the start of the year, the aid delivered shot up and almost met the target set. And by the end of the year, sufficient seed had been supplied to most parts of Bosnia to allow people to start planting their own crops again, and the number of people dependent on aid had fallen by a half. That's a result.

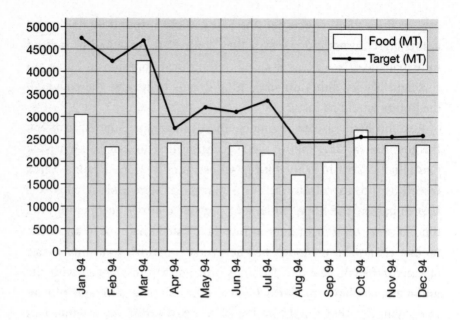

Working with the press

There's no doubt that Rose's clear strategic thinking and his courage to implement the strategy, despite advice from top UN bureaucrats who believed it impossible, fed and watered and clothed many people who might otherwise have perished in the winter of 1994–95. But UNPROFOR wasn't operating in a vacuum, and Rose understood that in order to win the support of the international community he needed to communicate to the world that they were successfully turning a failing humanitarian mission into a winning one. For that, the press was to play a vital role.

When Rose arrived in Sarajevo in January 1994, journalists were banned from the UN headquarters and from travelling in UN vehicles. In what might have been considered a high-risk policy, Rose turned this on its head and threw open the doors of the Residency to journalists. Next door to Rose's small office on the first floor was a large briefing room that rapidly became the nerve centre of his command organization in Bosnia; over time it developed the atmosphere of a university common room, as people came and went and new ideas were debated.

Rose and his team often drew on the knowledge and experience of the journalists, as many of them had been in Bosnia since the outbreak of war and had a greater understanding of the causes of the conflict. But the flow of information worked the other way as well. By giving journalists access to UN communications and allowing them to talk directly to those involved in running operations, Rose and his team were able to correct much of the hostile propaganda that had surrounded the UN mission. On one occasion, Jim Muir, foreign correspondent for the *Daily Telegraph*, ambled into the outer office while Rose was talking to the commander of the UN detachment in Bihac, which was under a severe Serb attack at the time. When Muir asked Rose what he was saying, Rose handed him the phone. 'Ask him yourself,' he said. Muir's report the next day was a great deal more balanced than those in any other newspaper covering the crisis.

The importance of getting accurate information

Rose would argue that whether at war, on a peacekeeping mission, or indeed in running an international business, without intelligence and information you are powerless. Unless you have a true understanding of what is really happening on the ground, it is impossible to come up with a realistic response. In a three-way civil war, establishing the facts could be a very difficult task indeed, and communicating them to the wider world could be even harder, particularly when there were certain things people simply didn't want to believe.

Rose describes how on 9 March 1994, General John Galvin, special adviser to President Clinton, arrived in Sarajevo tasked with bringing the Croat and Bosnian armies into a new federal defence structure. It was a crucially important visit. For the first time a senior US general would be able to see for himself the situation on the ground and the dangers Rose believed inherent in the policies apparently advocated in the USA by the State Department. The two men discussed the desire of the US State Department to enforce a 'just' solution in Bosnia and the consequences of the 'lift and strike' option so favoured by Congress. Congress wanted to lift the 1991 UN arms embargo to allow the poorly armed Bosnian Muslims to arm with imported weapons, and also wanted to launch air strikes against the Bosnian Serb army. As a military man, Galvin understood that the fighting ability of the Bosnian army wasn't merely determined by the size of its armoury. It would take years for the Bosnians to receive sufficient training and to acquire the necessary command discipline to fight successfully at a strategic level. By its very presence, the UN mission had prevented military defeat and preserved the State of Bosnia, and to withdraw it would be to drag America into war in support of the Bosnians.

The following day, Rose took Galvin to see the commander of the 2nd Bosnian Corps near Tuzla. They were accompanied by a member of staff from the US embassy, who in every discussion insisted on referring to the Serbs as 'the criminal and illegal regime of the Karadžić Montenegrin Serbs' and protested strongly if Rose referred to them simply as Serbs, wasting a great deal of time during meetings.

As they flew north to Tuzla on a clear, crisp winter's morning, this individual pointed down at destroyed villages dotted high in the Zvijezda Mountains beneath them and exclaimed to Galvin, 'Look at what the criminal Serbs have done!' Each time, Rose's military assistant Simon Shadbolt had to point out to Galvin that, actually, as the mosques in the area were still standing while the churches in the neighbouring villages had been destroyed, it was the Muslim forces that had been responsible for most of the ethnic cleansing in this particular region of Bosnia. It became obvious to Galvin that this representative from the State Department was simply not prepared to accept the idea that the Bosnians, as well as the Serbs, had been involved in any form of ethnic cleansing – a point that was only to be reinforced at the end of the day as they stood in Mostar, evidence of the worst devastation of the war all around them, when the State Department representative exclaimed, 'Well, at least *this* was done by the criminal Serbs.' Simon couldn't resist replying, 'Wrong again, this was done by the other half of your federation, the Croats.'

The best of all options to nail down the truth is, of course, to witness what is going on first-hand. But it is in nobody's power to be everywhere all the time. At the start of Rose's service in Bosnia, he was largely reliant on the United Nations Military Observers (UNMOs), a group established at the start of the first UN mission in Palestine in 1948. They were an unlikely group of people, purportedly from the sea, air and land forces of the UN member states and, with the odd exception, Rose wasn't impressed. It seemed to him that some took the job for the sizeable UN allowances, while others were billeted with local military commanders and, as a result, couldn't be relied upon for the impartiality of their reports. There was one UNMO in Goražde who rarely left the vaults of the bank he sheltered in when there was shelling in the streets. He gave graphic descriptions of what was going on outside and how the bank was under heavy fire, yet when Rose visited, its glass windows were intact and there was no damage to the building whatsoever.

To counteract the unhelpfulness of the UNMOS, Rose raised a new group of military liaison officers and observers called the Joint Commission Officers (JCOs), whose job was to be his eyes and ears in the field, as well as liaising on his behalf with the military commanders of the warring parties. In order to make timely, relevant decisions, Rose considered these eyes and ears on the ground as essential for being able to see through the mass of disinformation that poured out from the propaganda machines of the combatants.

The JCOs – selected for their personal qualities and language skills, and drawn from across the UN contingents under Rose's control in Bosnia – undoubtedly provided Rose with more reliable information about what was happening in the crisis areas of Bosnia, and proved of vital importance to the UN internationally as well. For example, sometimes Kofi Annan would be on the telephone from New York about a developing situation in Bosnia, armed only with patchy reports from UNMOs. On such occasions, the JCOs' eyewitness accounts from the frontline would prove critical in providing Annan with an accurate picture of what was going on. The JCOs' headquarters were located in the Residency, right next to the NATO air cell, and Rose could talk to both units through the open window of his office, at the same time if need be – a means by which he was sometimes found directing air strikes in defence of the convoys he was so determined would reach the suffering civilians caught in the Bosnian conflict.

Results of a year in Bosnia

To conclude, the first and most crucial element of Rose's strategy was the delivery of humanitarian aid on which so many people's lives depended. From a failing mission at the start, Rose turned this around so that with the delivery of seed as well as food meant that the number of people dependent on aid fell by half by the end of his year in command. The second element was the creation of conditions for the political settlement of the war. Rose worked hard at this, making every effort to dig deep for the truth, and negotiating with political and military figures on all three sides of the conflict as well as representatives from the international community, but a lasting settlement was going to prove elusive.

At the end of Rose's year in Bosnia, the republic was still at war. Throughout his 12 months in Bosnia, Rose had repeatedly peddled the same line over and over again: that the UN was in Bosnia for humanitarian reasons. 'We are not here to fight a war,' he said. 'We are here working for the people of this country, impartially.' This, after all, had been the consensus among all the UN ambassadors around the table in Sir David Hannay's elegant New York apartment. But a call for firmer action that had been there from the beginning, and that Rose had managed to suppress for a very long while, gradually became louder as time passed. Madeleine Albright, who signed up to the coalition established around the table in New York, and who was in agreement with Rose in conversations she had with him directly, was nonetheless in favour publicly of a 'lift and strike' policy. It became increasingly clear that the Americans wished for the 'just' solution and were prepared to take military action in order to ensure it.

Rose had both supporters and critics, depending on which side their sympathies lay. There were officials in Clinton's administration, inclined to support the Bosnian Muslims, who acknowledged that Rose performed a service by calming the conflict in the Sarajevo region, while there were others in Washington who grew increasingly angry with him over what they saw as his obstruction of a tougher line with the Serbs. General Bertrand de Lapresle, the French UN commander for former Yugoslavia, praised him highly: 'He has remained steadfastly loyal to the principle of peacekeeping, applying the relevant UN mandates with vigour and impartiality.'

Rose was very clear on this last point: a UN peacekeeping mission could not be dragged into a war. In his words, 'It would have to be another force that came here to do that.' But equally, he said, 'In the final analysis, as peacekeepers, we cannot enforce the end of fighting, and if one side or the other determines to go back to a policy of war, there is very little we can do about it, other than point out the likely consequences of their actions and decisions that will be visited on the heads of their people.'

At the end of the day, Rose successfully created a coalition, forged a clear path through the fog of war, and turned a failing humanitarian mission into one that successfully delivered aid to thousands of people who otherwise would have perished. He's a man with a strong moral compass, who sleeps well at night, who courageously put the task of helping people in need above his own personal safety. His clear thinking and focus on the objective, and his ability to turn strategy into action and effectively implement change (despite resistance from within the organization in which he was operating) is a skill that could be productively employed in many organizations, private and public.

The one thing beyond Rose's control – indeed beyond anybody's control – is the persistent use of lies and propaganda which might be considered a legitimate weapon of war but is at play in the world of business and corporations as well, though one hopes not to such an extent. The lessons Rose learned about the information battle in Bosnia, that might be equally valid in business, are as follows:

1) Strive to have a complete understanding of the reality of a situation. In Rose's case, he achieved this as far as it was possible through the employment of the JCOs.

2) Create the means by which you can put the record straight, rather than allowing propaganda to prevail. Rose opened the doors of the Residency to the press, and repeatedly pushed the message of the UN's impartiality and humanitarian role.

3) Don't believe the propaganda against you, or indeed your own propaganda. Everything must be based on reality, not on rhetoric.

4) If there are difficult questions to answer, or a record to set straight, send out your top person. Fail to do this and the top person won't survive.

5) Work ahead of time and be aware of the environment in which you're working.

Rose might also have added: develop the skin of a rhinoceros. Raise your head above the parapet and there will always be people who throw accusations at you. At one point, Rose was accused by the US General Wesley Clark of suffering from Stockholm syndrome, suggesting he had developed a psychological alliance with his captors as a survival strategy – his captors, of course, being the Serbs. Rose had to point out to General Clark that this just wasn't the case. UNPROFOR was following a neutral line. It wasn't General Wesley's line, but they weren't about to shift.

Two years on, there were still efforts being made to discredit UNPROFOR and Rose as its commander. One afternoon Rose was tending his garden at his home in Dorset when the phone rang and, in Rose's words, 'a rather chilly voiced brigadier who I knew in the Ministry of Defence said to me, "There are reports coming in from various newspapers of you having been photographed coming out of a brothel in Sarajevo. What have you got to say to that?" Well, I put on a pretty chilly voice myself and said, "OK, you should read your history, brigadier, the same accusation was made against one of my predecessors, and as a result I never went out of base without keeping a minute-by-minute diary of where we were and what we were doing, and never went out with not one but two people. So can you tell me *which* day you are talking about?" That's how bad it gets.'

Reassuring, then, to walk through Hyde Park a decade later and be approached by a group of men who recognized him from Sarajevo. 'They were locals in Sarajevo at the time – might have been from any side of the conflict,' said Rose, 'and they said, "Thank God you didn't listen to the propaganda, because it was you – the UN – that kept us alive."'

CHAPTER THREE

A Challenge of Implementing Change in Government

In any merger, the biggest challenge is always integration of human resources because the people who are coming in have a lot of apprehension.

Arundhati Bhattacharya, former chair of the State Bank of India

In the UK, the Department for International Trade aims to secure prosperity by promoting and financing international trade and investment, and championing free trade. Prior to the Department for International Trade, it was UK Trade & Investment that carried out a similar role, and prior to UK Trade & Investment, it was British Trade International. During this time, the development of one governmental department into another represented gentle evolutionary steps in international trade and investment, and at each point the role was fulfilled by one single department.

Prior to British Trade International, however, the role of promoting British trade was carried out not by one but by two government departments: the Foreign & Commonwealth Office and the Department of Trade and Industry. Bringing together the promotion of British trade into a single governmental body involved merging two extremely different workplace cultures and presented the monumental challenge of implementing change in an atmosphere that might be described at best as 'resistant'.

The man employed for the job was British diplomat Sir David Wright, then serving as the ambassador to Japan. The starting point was when Tony Blair set up an examination in 1997 of the way in which Britain promoted trade. The resulting Wilson Review recommended the formation of a new government department: British Trade International. And in 1999, Wright was, in his words, 'hauled out of Tokyo to be its chief executive and set it up'. He adds without hesitation, 'It was the most difficult job I did in 36 years of public service.'

Difficulties merging two departments

One of the problems in setting up what was effectively a hybrid government department was that Wright reported to the Foreign Secretary on one hand and the Secretary of State for Trade and Industry on the other, which in his words was 'not brilliant in terms of organization'. More difficult still, both departments and both permanent secretaries saw his appointment partially as a threat to their turf and partially as an opportunity to enlarge their turf. 'There was an execution issue that was of massive proportions,' says Wright. The merger represented a major transformational change in the way the government did something, and yet it was dealt with as if it were 'just another civil service job'. He adds, 'There was no preparation, no training, nothing. Just here you are, this is the job, here's the report, implement it.'

Wright argues that the government was behind the curve in terms of 'preparedness' then, as indeed it was more recently with Brexit. Wright refers to David Cameron's refusal, prior to the referendum of 23 June 2016, to allow the civil service to do any scenario 'gaming' of what might happen in the event that the British public voted to leave the EU, because Cameron was so committed to staying and didn't wish it to be known that the government was preparing for any other possibility.

There is no doubt that 'gaming' in the case of Brexit, just like providing training and advice on executing strategy in the case of creating a new hybrid government department, would have been a sensible and productive approach. But as Wright concludes, 'one just accepted it as another job, and it was only in the course of the process that one started thinking that it could be beneficial to have some advice.'

As someone whose experience has spanned both the public and private sectors, both in Britain and overseas, Wright is of the view that one of the most serious failings of British society has been the lack of integration between the public and private sectors, as well as between different parts of the public sector, and that there are many lessons to be learned.

'The public sector,' he says, 'curiously is the antithesis of what the popular impression might be; it is much more ruthless, with more internal competition, than one might think. There is one simple reason for this. If you are in the public sector, your only road to success is up the greasy pole. Everyone is graded and there is no financial incentive for success; it's promotion that gets you into more influential positions, and you can only move between departments with great difficulty. What's more,' he adds, 'the diplomatic service is based upon a separate administrative order in council to the home civil service, so theoretically they are separate organizations with separate heads and separate methodologies.'

Acquisitions and mergers can be challenging enough in the private sector, fraught as they can be with difficulties in fusing different corporate cultures and ways of doing things. In the public sector, the rigid departmental structure only accentuates the problem. Both the Foreign Commonwealth Office (FCO) and the Department of Trade and Industry (DTI) had their own respective organizations for promoting trade and investment, and Wright's job was to extract these departments from the DTI and FCO and bring them together under one umbrella. 'Two groups,' he says, 'each with different levels of antipathy to the other, and with deep personal sentiments.'

'At the start,' says Wright, 'the DTI resisted the government review, and the members of the department dealing with export promotion were suspicious about what the outcome would be. They saw two threats. First, they saw export promotion being taken away from the DTI and put into this new government department. And secondly, they saw the prospect of their own career progression facing impediments, which they hadn't previously thought that they would face.'

Inevitably, there was also a perceived sense of superiority on the part of the Foreign Office. The DTI civil servants felt those in the diplomatic service regarded themselves as a cut above them, in part encouraged by the sentiment that a diplomat's status is to some extent more recognized in British society than that of a civil servant working in Victoria Street, and also by the belief among those working overseas that they were at the sharp end of the business. Diplomats overseas were directly involved with potential opportunities for exporting British goods, whereas the people in the DTI, in their view, were sitting comfortably at their desks pushing paper.

Add to this the thorny issue that Wright himself was a diplomat. No matter that his extensive experience in both change management and trade and investment promotion made him the right man for the job; his appointment was simultaneously a victory for the FCO and a threat for the home civil servants in the DTI. Playground politics, one might think, but gritty enough when squeezed into an inflexible structure that requires individuals to defend their own patch.

In addition to the FCO and DTI, Wright had a third group to manage as well: the Regional Development Agencies across the UK. These included regional authorities – such as Yorkshire and Humber, East Anglia, South West England – and the devolved administrations: Scotland, Wales and Northern Ireland, all important in the overall package of promoting UK trade. They were local governmental bodies answerable to local representatives, but were in a sense caught between the FCO and DTI, in that they were largely dependent on the DTI for funding, and at the same time needed to ensure that if, for example, they sent a trade mission to Saudi Arabia, the FCO representative in Saudi Arabia was approached in a way that encouraged maximum assistance to the exporters of their particular region.

Importance of communication

So how did Wright forge together 3,000 or so public servants in three disparate groups to work collectively toward the common goal of promoting British trade? Especially when one of the groups felt extraordinarily threatened by the process – and when none of the groups welcomed change?

The answer, in a single word, is communication – an overload of communication.

'I used to travel around the country a lot, and internationally,' says Wright, 'maintaining a position of visibility vis-à-vis both our staff and our clients, explaining what we were doing, and seeking to secure their support for this unified government department.'

'Another thing which I attach great importance to was the personal attempt to ensure that every day I was in the office, I tried at some point to carve out half an hour to go down to one of the floors of the building and show my face, talk to people and give them a sense that the CEO was an accessible person – a real person – who was interested in what they were up to.'

'In an effort to make a single integrated entity,' Wright says, 'I also tried to encourage those people who effectively had been home department civil servants, who were now in this hybrid organization, to do some of the work of those who lived abroad. I offered them the opportunity to get jobs overseas in embassies, dealing with the promotion of British exports in those markets. The postings were from two to five years and a lot of them took it up.' Admittedly this policy created a few ripples in the Foreign Office, but Wright argues that 'in any large organization there is always a way you can manage a percentage of people who are transiting between one role to another; it's not impossible to do that.'

Working with those who resisted change

There was one problem, however, that was insurmountable. 'I don't think anybody outside the government services realizes how hard it is to sack somebody,' Wright says. 'It is really tough. And yet there were people working in London in the head office who were viscerally opposed to what we were trying to do. This was one of the things I ran up against which caused me to have great doubts about how the public sector is managed in this country, to the extent that over the period of three and half years when I did the job, I seriously considered resigning a number of times.'

'There's an interesting management issue here, which I think is a broader one,' says Wright. 'Does one manage by "bust up", and blow the whole thing sky high by publicizing your dissatisfaction, or does one manage "around a situation"? I think that all managers come up against this dilemma. A lot depends on the inherent nature and character of the people involved.' Though clearly frustrated at times, Wright says, 'I'm by nature somebody who manages around things, and would willingly confess that. If it hadn't been clear to me before this particular exercise, it became very clear afterwards. I simply believe that one has got to do the job and one's therefore got to try to manage around it.'

The simple fact in the civil service, and many large corporations as well, is that there is no choice, unless you wish to throw in the towel and resign and effectively give up on the mission. So sticking with the job and learning to work around the recalcitrants becomes an important skill.

Wright draws on one example, which would be easy to imagine as a sketch in the BBC's political satire *Yes Minister.* When British Trade International was initially created, it was specifically for the promotion of British trade overseas, not for inward investors to the UK. 'This to me, and to many people, was a nonsense,' says Wright. About a year and half into the job, Wright, together with the minister responsible for trade and investment promotion and a senior official had a meeting to discuss integrating investment promotion alongside trade promotion under the British Trade International banner. At one point in the conversation, after the discussion had been going round in circles for some while, the minister said, 'Well look, it's so logical to bring investment promotion alongside trade promotion, why on earth wasn't this done when the Wilson Report was produced?'

To which the official responded, 'Because I didn't want it.'

The minister responded to the official, 'But I'm the minister, you're the official.'

The response came, 'I know you are, Minister, but what you do on my watch, you do on my advice.'

So, one individual had the power to block an entirely commonsensical policy that would have benefitted the country's trade and prosperity.

Not so very long after this meeting, Wright succeeded, through well-honed diplomatic and influencing skills, to persuade an official in Number 10 that this change should take place, who in turn persuaded the prime minister. Thus by the latter half of 2001, the people responsible for inward investment promotion joined forces with the people responsible for trade promotion in British Trade International – a success, but one that Wright readily admits would have been considerably more difficult had officials not changed. 'The phrase that I frequently found myself using,' says Wright, 'was that I spent three years fighting battles in Whitehall and not doing any trade promotion at all.'

As time went on, though, Wright discovered a talent for selecting fights that he had a fair chance of winning, which left time and energy for new initiatives. British Trade International was a leading governmental department in establishing an external private sector board, which included representatives of different UK companies – British Oxygen, for example, and Rolls Royce – as well as companies from the SME sector, in order to listen to the business world and learn what it wanted from this new business department. He also introduced a system where the regular appraisal process of the people doing the trade and investment promotion work at a senior level, particularly those overseas, had two parts to it. So, every UK ambassador or high commissioner who had a trade and investment promotion responsibility reported not only to the head of the Foreign Office but also to Wright himself as chief executive of British Trade International. 'I think they were a little surprised they had to satisfy me, as well as the conventional reporting lines, that they were doing the job they were supposed to do,' says Wright. 'It woke them up a bit, let's put it that way.'

The alignment of the two governmental departments working together under the British Trade Investment umbrella, and motivating those who resisted change, was always going to be the biggest challenge. Wright estimates that 60–65 per cent of the 3,000 or so civil servants employed in the FCO and DTI were prepared to accept the need for change, while 30–35 per cent were resistant. Sir David was a firm believer in the project and conveyed the message passionately, but without power to hire and fire, the only alternative was to manage the situation in the best way possible.

'One made it clear that we were doing what ministers had asked for, and what the prime minister had instructed to be done,' says Wright, 'and that many of us were committed to the outcome and that we were just going to go on. I was a member of the managing boards of both departments – the FCO managing board and the DTI managing board – and got a fair hearing from both sides.' As 'the man from the Foreign Office', it was always going to be easier to win support from the FCO, but Wright says it helped that 'the DTI was run by a man called Michael Scholar. Michael was fair. He didn't much like what was having to be done but, like good public servants, he recognized that's what the ministers had decided, and they had to get on with it.'

The fact was, the 'resistant third' got on with the job the way they'd always done it. 'I'd give them 60 per cent for getting on with it,' says Wright, 'but they never had that extra 40 per cent of commitment and drive that you'd like. Because one couldn't get rid of them, one supported their continuation while limiting the damage, and as time went on, the recalcitrants were reduced in number.'

To measure the success of British Trade International in terms of increased trade is, in Wright's view, impossible. 'There is,' he says, 'a scandalous and very ignorant wish on the part of politicians to be able to do it, but civil servants hold their heads in horror.' Too many variables, too difficult to disaggregate elements of compound products constructed in multiple countries, too subject to macroeconomic fluctuations. And if it's difficult to measure trade, it's even more so to measure the effects of promotion on trade.

Nonetheless, the response to British Trade International was positive. British exporters and members of parliament welcomed the fact that a sensible approach had been adopted, as did Regional Development Agencies and Chambers of Commerce across the country. It was the big merger that led to a number of little steps that created the Department for International Trade we have today.

The road to this successful outcome might have felt unsettling, disruptive and even threatening to some, but the reality in today's world is that change is a constant and we have a choice to resist it or to embrace it. Resistance isn't a path to success, however. As Darwin discovered a long while ago, it is the adaptable that survive. Looking forward, all indicators suggest that the pace of change is only going to increase, and arguably we should be arming our young people with the tools to be resilient to change so they can flourish. By circumstance rather than design, Covid might have offered something of a silver lining in this regard. Young people across the world have been forced to ask questions never asked before: Will I be going to school next term? Will I be sitting external exams this summer? How do I navigate this very difficult and constantly shifting situation?

Despite the 'resistant third', as Wright refers to those reluctant to accept change, he stuck to his guns and, as should be the goal of every leader, he pursued what he knew to be right. It was clearly in the interests of the country to have a joined-up approach to trade. We see here that it is a leader's role to set the tone and communicate the big picture in order to inspire, encourage and persuade those in their teams to follow suit and make the right calls. Arguably, it is easier and more engaging to follow a strategy that is just and rational. But if all fails, a leader with a true sense of purpose will stick to his or her guns anyway, and find a way to manage and work around those reluctant to change their ways.

CHAPTER FOUR

Transforming Education
for the Better

*Education is simply the soul of a society as it passes from one generation
to another.*

G. K. Chesterton, writer, philosopher and poet

To stand even a chance of comprehending the complexities of the
current British education system, it is a prerequisite to understand
the history of the British Isles over the last millennium, for today
we are living with the residual legacies of a yesteryear divided by
class, money, religion, gender and the postcode lottery. There are a
handful of exemplary schools held in such high regard that they are
sought after by parents the world over, and other schools that are
frankly unfit for purpose. In 2018, well over a quarter of 16-year-
olds failed to achieve the 'standard' Grade 4 GCSEs in English and
Maths that are required to secure the vast majority of jobs, do an
apprenticeship or to go on to further education.[1] Like the London
Underground, the education system is too difficult to modernize
all at once – and generally, it can be argued, has been somewhat
resistant to change. Yet here we look at two individuals, one in the
state sector and one in the independent sector, both recognized and
decorated for their contributions to education, whose strongly held

beliefs, dedication and irrepressible energy have benefitted hundreds of thousands of young people.

Aged 62, following a successful career as Chief Education Officer in both Oxfordshire's and Birmingham's local authorities, Sir Tim Brighouse was begged to give up any idea of retirement and accept a post as Schools Commissioner for London. There he would lead the *London Challenge*, which, in the years 2002–07, transformed failing secondary schools the length and breadth of the capital into thriving communities of learning where parents felt it a privilege to send their children.

In January 2006, author, historian and educationalist Sir Anthony Seldon took on the headship of Wellington College – a once prestigious public school steeped in military history that had lost favour to competing schools, with the number of pupils falling well below capacity – and totally transformed it to the point that aspiring families were queuing at the gates. After seven years of Seldon's leadership, in 2013 readers of *The Week* magazine voted Wellington College 'the most forward-thinking school in the UK' and upmarket *Tatler* magazine voted it 'the best senior school in Britain'.

Both Brighouse and Seldon lived and breathed education. Both studied at Oxford, both were schoolteachers first, then deputy heads – and then their career paths diverged. Seldon went on to be headmaster at St Dunstan's College in South London, then Brighton College and finally Wellington College, while Brighouse moved into local education authorities.

Sir Tim Brighouse

'I have always thought there is no more important job in life than teaching, because you unlock kids,' says Brighouse. 'A teacher is a key to a civilized community and to social justice. We've just got to learn and learn, and learn from our mistakes as well,' he says, and not just while at school. 'A good teacher,' he says, 'a *good* teacher,' emphasizing his point, 'will say, "you've made a mistake, wonderful! Now we've got something to work with..."'

Brighouse speaks of one of his own mistakes as if it were yesterday: a couple of terms into his job in Oxfordshire, 'the head of Didcot Girls' School, Jenny Cottee, came to me and said "you're not a very good communicator". She seemingly jolted Brighouse into action.

'Communication – you can't overdo it,' he says. 'And there are no shortcuts; it has to be personal. You have to accept that if you're running a very large organization you will necessarily be a remote leader – people aren't going to see you that often. People won't hear; they won't listen. People come anew to the organization. How do you deal with induction? How do you help people get on board?'

'I used to write letters to people on Friday evenings,' he says. 'Hundreds of letters, handwritten. I would get people in the system to give me names of people who were exceptionally committed – those who had walked the extra mile – then I would write to them, something along the lines, "Jim Smith was telling me about your amazing commitment in doing such and such at the school and I just wanted you to know how fortunate we are to have somebody like you." By mentioning somebody else in the letter, it had a double effect.'

He also made a deliberate effort to write numerous articles and books, emulating thought leader and headteacher Michael Marland, who Brighouse observed was repeatedly able to recruit the very best teachers to his school on the strength of his reputation acquired through the written word. In further efforts to attract the best, Brighouse would accept invitations to speak to groups of teachers around the country. It mattered not that it was on the weekend. And every evening he'd share a meal with half a dozen people – a different half dozen every night – at one or another Indian restaurant. 'I used to call it "putting on the sticky stuff",' he says.

Difficult not to ask about his family life; did he have time for one? He is married to the Labour leader of Oxfordshire County Council, Liz Brighouse, who also leads a crazily busy life. When they were about to get married, she was quoted in the local papers as saying, 'Some people live together and don't get married, but we are going to get married but not live together.'

'It isn't easy, you can't do it with anything less than total commitment,' says Brighouse. 'The obligations just multiply.' After 10 years in the Oxfordshire post, Brighouse had reached the point where he felt guilty taking time out to read the Sunday papers – and left to become Professor of Education at Keele University. He regretted it within a month. He'd absolutely loved his job in Oxfordshire and wondered why on earth he had given it up. 'I thought I was burned out,' he says, 'but actually I just needed a holiday.'

Working for Birmingham Local Authority

This point of self-reflection is one that Brighouse quickly turned to his advantage. He was at Keele for four years, during which he carried out research and read extensively, honing his understanding of school improvement. And then, in his words, he got his lucky break. In his early 50s, in 1993 he was appointed Chief Education Officer of Birmingham Local Authority. Times were different then. 'It seemed I was the only person who thought that the role of the local authority was to improve schools,' says Brighouse.

He had quite a challenge on his hands. At the time of his appointment, Birmingham was declared by the Conservative Secretary of State for Education, John Patten, as the worst local education authority in the country. Brighouse recalls encountering the desperate phrase, 'What more can you expect from kids from backgrounds like this?' The teachers were demoralized – a culture Brighouse felt compelled to shift.

Being firm about what you stand for and creating a strong sense of community are two ideals that resonate strongly with Brighouse. He was once invited to take on a leading role in social services in Birmingham and declined, on the basis that he had never been a social worker and didn't believe he could be a credible leader.

'My community was teachers and schools,' he says. 'I was always speculating about what schools were up to, what was their purpose? I wasn't telling them what to do. That's very unusual in the schooling system, but absolutely crucial – I want *them* thinking, I don't want to tell them what to think.'

He slotted straight into the teaching community in Birmingham in part because of what might have been considered a rather unfortunate incident. On hearing that Brighouse had been appointed the job, John Patten, who had known him from his Oxfordshire days, described Brighouse as 'a madman....wandering the street, frightening the children'. Brighouse sued and won substantial damages, which he donated to inner-city educational charities. But the consequences reached beyond that. John Patten wasn't a popular man in the teaching community, and as a result, Brighouse found support. 'People were with me from the beginning. Even though they didn't know me, they felt they knew me,' he says.

In the first three months, Brighouse ran a series of workshops on how to improve schools, each for about 30–35 people. These were first aimed at primary schools and then at secondary schools. Haim Ginott, the child psychologist, once said of being a teacher, 'I have come to the frightening conclusion: I am the decisive element in the classroom. It is my personal approach that creates the climate. It is my daily mood that makes the weather.' Heads of department and subject leaders also affect the 'weather' for the students, and then headteachers affect the 'weather' within which the individual teachers work.

Brighouse ran his first workshop for the newest heads in Birmingham: those more likely to spread a positive message. The cynics and old stagers he left until last. (The importance of communication again.) 'By the way,' he adds, 'I identified about five naysayer heads who nevertheless had strong voices. If I were to be writing a paper for the committee, I would nip round to the school where the naysayer was and say, "Jim, in total confidence, could you possibly read this and tell me what I've got wrong."'

With a strongly held view that learning is for life, Brighouse continued to develop his own skills as he made every effort to develop the skills of others. The senior leadership team in Birmingham employed a coach. 'He would always bring me something of interest to read,' says Brighouse, 'the most impressive being an article by Cooperrider and Srivastva on "appreciative enquiry" and problem-solving – tremendously important.' Put simply, 'appreciative enquiry' correctly identifies what someone has done well. Like a good teacher, it says, 'this bit is really, really good'. It opens people up and stimulates enquiry for better practice; it creates a vision of what will be. Problem-solving, on the other hand, identifies a problem, analyses the causes, brainstorms for possible solutions, and develops an action plan. Cooperrider and Srivastva argued that you need three parts of appreciative enquiry for every one part of problem-solving, if only because people need the boost in energy and self-belief that appreciative enquiry provides. There are problems enough and they have to be solved, but they require energy and persistence.

'Incidentally,' say Brighouse, 'my coach told me I was all right on the appreciative enquiry and I was all right on the problem-solving, but I wasn't quite as good at differentiating which problems to solve and in what order – which I found immensely helpful.'

Tim Brighouse was Chief Education Officer in Birmingham for 10 years, and in that time he completely turned the culture on its head. No more defeatist grumbling about 'kids from backgrounds like this'. 'The nicest thing any councillor said to me,' Brighouse reflects, 'is that they had been speaking to a teacher at some social gathering or other, who had moved from London to teach in Birmingham. When the councillor asked why, the teacher said because everybody knew that if you wanted to succeed in education and teaching, you'd better teach in Birmingham where all the action was. We became a magnet for ever better people.'

Ever better people meant ever better teaching and ever better results. After Brighouse's appointment in 1993, results across the city improved year on year at every level and at a faster rate than national averages. At Key Stage 2, 71 per cent achieved Level 4 or above in English in 2001, compared with 46 per cent in 1996; in Maths, 67 per cent compared with 44 per cent; and in Science, 85 per cent compared with 48 per cent. And in the same year of 2001, 41.4 per cent of pupils achieved five or more A to C grades at GCSE, compared to 33 per cent in 1996. Brighouse took an underperforming service and transformed it into a service with an international reputation for excellent education. No wonder then that politicians were begging him to do the same in London.

Working in London

It was in early 2002 that the then Secretary of State, Estelle Morris, first suggested that a focused effort on London secondary schools might be desirable. There was already a general consensus among politicians and journalists that London state schools, particularly secondary schools, were places to be avoided if you wanted a good education for your children, and statistics appeared to support this: 13 per cent of secondary school children living in the capital attended private schools, compared with 7 per cent nationally[2], in part because of a dissatisfaction with the state sector. There was nothing new in this; it had been the case at least since the 1960s. Statistics showed that in 1989, fewer than 9 per cent of Inner London secondary school pupils achieved five or more higher grades at GCSE, compared with 17 per cent nationally.[3] It wasn't difficult to secure the agreement of the prime minister, Tony Blair, whose own difficulties in securing a London state secondary school place for his eldest son had been widely publicized. And so the London Challenge was born.

It is extraordinary that a man in his sixty-third year, mentally preparing for retirement, should muster the energy to start afresh, and on a project of such massive scale – made possible, surely, by the fact that he was driven by a moral purpose. Brighouse had the belief and the experience to transform London schools, and the politicians knew it. Much of what he was able to implement in London was tried and honed in Birmingham and Oxfordshire before that – though Brighouse is very clear that it is critical to understand different contexts and adapt accordingly.

In Birmingham, for example, he knew that the press was on his side and that he could communicate successfully to a wide audience through radio and television – in part because of John Patten's slandering. London was different; the media was less likely to be on board. Brighouse chose his tribe carefully and deliberately located himself in the Institute of Education, knowing this to be highly regarded by teachers, rather than in the Department for Education, which might be less than highly regarded by teachers. He considered it helpful, too, that he had spent a couple of years as deputy in the London Education Authority early in his career, and that a lot of young teachers he had met then, now in positions of leadership, would consider him 'one of them', at least in part overcoming any prejudice that may have arisen from an outsider coming into the city to impose change.

Brighouse explains that the essence of the London Challenge involved an exercise in bringing about change for the better in a very loosely organized schooling system. At its heart was a culture shift, in part at the Department for Education and Skills (DFES), which was funding and orchestrating the change, but principally in schools and classrooms where improvements would have an immediate impact on children and their education. 'Teachers and their school leaders have to be driven by a moral purpose, and certainty of pupils' success that brooks no denial,' says Brighouse. 'Without that, nothing exceptional will happen.' How that is communicated and shared is elusive, but Brighouse believes that to be successful, complex cultural change of this sort needs to be underpinned by a grasp of three elements.

First, any intervention needs to allow for differences in context. Brighouse was acutely aware of the different approaches required in two major cities in England, as expressed above, but he argues that there are key differences in individual schools, boroughs and socio-economic groups that need to be understood as well – and the strategy tweaked accordingly.

Secondly, it is helpful to have a shared map and language – in this case of 'school improvement' – so there's less chance of misunderstanding when people are trying to learn from each other. 'I argued strongly for this,' says Brighouse. 'It was vital to realize that in everything we said, wrote or did, we were conveying an impression either positive or negative to staff in schools on whom we relied entirely to achieve anything.'

On Brighouse's arrival in London, some schools were in a 'special measures' Ofsted category. These schools were failing, but Brighouse argued that to label them 'failing' – or worse, by the derogatory phrase 'sink schools' – was unlikely to motivate them to improve. 'It isn't that you shouldn't confront failure: of course you should,' he says, 'but surely in the context of giving those schools the benefit of the doubt, you should assume they start from a position of wanting to succeed.' As such he argued they should be called 'keys to success', since if they could succeed – and lift themselves from the bottom of the pecking order of parental preference – then any school could and should succeed.

Thirdly, there is the need to recognize that change often falters because of failure in communication. Brighouse learned this early in his career. He threw everything he had at it, yet concluded that any leader of complex change has to calmly accept that communication will fail from time to time and that it needs constant attention.

Constant attention is something he certainly gave. The scale of the London Challenge in sheer numbers was greater than anything he had done before: over 400 secondary schools, 32 boroughs and the DFES, plus a whole set of separate stakeholders such as politicians, headteachers, teachers, support staff, governors, civil servants and, of course, students and their parents – and that's before counting organizations that represented the various gatekeepers to these groups, such as the teacher unions, faith groups and employer groups.

Brighouse would spend hours with a map of all the schools and photographs of the heads, doing his homework, learning names and basic data about the schools before meeting people. The London Challenge was launched by the Prime Minister at The Globe in April 2003, but months beforehand a small unit of five 'fast track' civil servants, led by widely respected Cambridge Maths graduate and teacher Sir Jon Coles, had already begun work on how to allocate the budget. Coles' analysis of the data and the socio-economic background of London, together with a mutually agreed approach to school improvement across all the capital's secondary schools, formed the basis of what was to become the strategy for the London Challenge – and while this work was being carried out, Brighouse was in the habit of rising early and visiting schools. 'I visited 150 of the 400 secondary schools in six months,' he says. 'I'd spend three or four hours in each, following up with a letter to everybody I met that day, thanking them. I was perpetually communicating.'

There was recognition of a fourth element of successful change as well, and that was getting the right people, in the right place, doing the right things, at the right time. This would affect the running of all aspects of the London Challenge, including of course the schools themselves. Just as in Birmingham, 'one of our goals was to change the atmosphere so that people were attracted to teach in London, and then retained in London,' says Brighouse. 'That was a key part of the London Challenge.'

However, getting the right people in positions of leadership sometimes required tough measures. It generally involved restructuring, making people apply for jobs they didn't get. 'But,' says Brighouse, 'you can get many people on board who haven't been on board before, when deep down teaching is what they want to do but they may have become cynical because they've been badly led. You can change loads of things.'

The London Challenge had a big drive on improving school leadership; the National College for School Leadership was brought on board to place consultant heads – usually on a part-time basis – into schools that were underperforming.

Teacher development was also brought centre stage with the Chartered London Teacher initiative. 'I was of the view that if you are teaching in London you need to know more about pedagogy, more about your subject, more about overcoming barriers to kids learning, and you need to understand about different racial connotations because you're working with different races,' says Brighouse. Teachers were incentivized with an additional £1,000 to visit each other's schools and build up a portfolio of experience to extend their skills in these key areas. 'That was the big story of London,' says Brighouse. 'We overcame isolation and started to get people to work in partnership and learn from each other.'

This was done in an ingenious manner. Rather than schools learning from their immediate geographical neighbours – who after all were competing for the same pool of local children – they shared learning with schools in the same 'family of schools', divided and organized according to socio-economic background and peppered across the 32 London boroughs. This emulated methodology first practised in Birmingham, where 'family of schools' data sets were gathered and openly shared in full detail, so that schools could compare their performance against other schools in similar circumstances. It made it very easy to see if a school had fallen behind or if its performance had stagnated, or conversely if it had done comparatively well. The point of the 'family' is that schools were grouped with others that had similar prior entry attainment scores and similar numbers of pupils entitled to free school meals, so the comparison was relevant – they could visit and learn from schools they knew to be broadly similar.

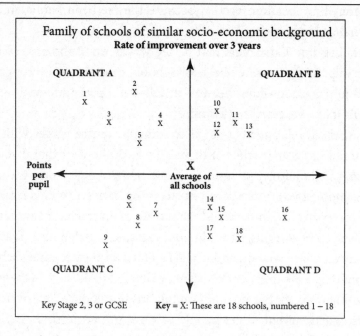

Family of schools of similar socio-economic background
Rate of improvement over 3 years

QUADRANT A   QUADRANT B

Points per pupil ← Average of all schools →

QUADRANT C   QUADRANT D

Key Stage 2, 3 or GCSE   **Key** = X: These are 18 schools, numbered 1 – 18

The graph above illustrates schools in the same family – in this case 18 of them – plotted on a graph with 'rate of improvement' on the vertical axis and 'points per pupil' attained at either Key Stage 2, Key Stage 3 or GCSE on the horizontal axis. The crossing of the axis marks the spot of the 'average of all schools'. Clearly schools in the bottom left-hand quadrant aren't improving as fast as other comparable schools – 'not waving but drowning,' Brighouse says with a smile. Schools in the top left corner are improving more quickly than comparable schools but have low points per pupil, maybe 'heads above water'. Schools in the top right corner have both high rates of improvement and high points per pupil: 'walking on water'. And finally schools in the bottom right quadrant have high points per pupil but lower rates of improvement than comparable schools, and are 'treading water'. The detail of every subject was added to the data and the figures made available as three-year rolling averages. With this knowledge in hand, heads and teachers were encouraged to make purposeful visits to learn from each other.

There was a small group of part-time advisers, too – 'our gnarled advisers', as Brighouse affectionately called them – who each brought with them a long and successful experience in schools. The leader of this group was David Woods, who had been chief adviser in Birmingham before taking on his role at the DFES. The group would meet weekly or fortnightly with Jon Coles and his team, and discuss the progress of individual schools and school improvement more generally. Here the shared map and language that Brighouse felt so strongly about meant that they were all on the same page. Essentially, Brighouse explains, they were involved in ongoing learning about seven processes which are the everyday life of schools, namely: leading creatively, managing effectively, reviewing, developing staff, creating an environment fit for learning, involving parents and the community, and of course teaching, learning and assessing.

There is no doubt that the London Challenge was a success. Brighouse focused exclusively on secondary schools and retired in 2007, just as the London Challenge turned its attention to primary schools as well, with David Woods taking on the leadership. The two men worked tirelessly and wrote many books on education together. This isn't the place to detail all of their collective thinking, but one theme worthy of note and which is of value to an audience wider than just schools is the 'butterfly effect' – so named from the chaos theory which suggests that the flap of a butterfly's wing in Brazil can set off a cascade of atmospheric events that, weeks later, spurs the formation of a tornado in Texas. Essentially it refers to low effort, high-impact things that make a huge difference. 'Teachers love them,' says Brighouse, as would anybody wanting to make a difference.

An example might be an 'achievement wall' at a primary school, with pictures of alumni who have passed through those same corridors before – engineers or writers or cracking good teachers – as role models for children who might not otherwise encounter them. Another example of a low-effort, high-impact change involves altering where pupils sit. Classroom layout – namely who sits next to whom – is often a source of pupil behaviour problems for the inexperienced or weaker teacher. Conscious of this, some schools insist on habitually changing the seating plan in a classroom in the first week of every half term so that it just becomes 'the way we do things here', and minor disruptions in the classroom are diminished as a result.

Does Brighouse feel the London Challenge has done its job? 'If you think you've arrived, you're done for,' he says, 'but we affected the culture. The culture was that London was a "sink" and that state schools were failing – that had been true for generations. Now the belief is – isn't it? – London schools are terrific.' But it will only be sustained for as long as London continues to attract and retain good teachers; otherwise it will just go through the floor again – a theme that crosses both the state and independent sectors.

Wellington College

Prior to Anthony Seldon's appointment, Wellington College had lost a bit of its fizz. It was a boys' public school, a stone's throw from the Royal Military Academy Sandhurst, formidable on the rugby pitch as well as in the arts, and prided itself on developing young men and women (girls had been admitted to the sixth form since the 1970s) who 'knew how to live'.

The number of pupils in the school was down (690 out of a capacity of 800), which is not good news for an independent school reliant on school fees for its survival. According to one of the housemasters, Neil Lunnon, the teaching staff were fiercely loyal but feeling increasingly disenchanted with the way things were going. 'I genuinely remember,' he says, 'doing a tour of the school with some prospective parents and wanting to whisper to them, *don't send your kids here – just at the moment, I wouldn't.* It was heart-breaking.'

So there was an urgent need for strong leadership and direction, and few doubted that Anthony Seldon – brilliant, strategic, brimming with drive and impatient energy – was the right man for the job. Just as there are soldiers who might be ordinary or even troublesome in peacetime but excel on the battlefield, so too with heads of schools. In Lunnon's words, 'Seldon was one of the most transformative individuals I have ever come across.'

Lunnon recalls that Seldon wasted no time at all in addressing the staff and spelling out exactly what they as a school community had to achieve. First, to become a great school again. That bit will be easy, he said. And secondly, to become distinctive. Seldon exuded a tremendous confidence that Wellington would indeed become a great school again, and quickly. Indeed, why on earth would it *not* be a great school, with its history and its facilities and its 400 acres of stunning parkland in luscious, leafy Berkshire?

In line with a trend that was sweeping across England, Seldon introduced the International Baccalaureate as an option alongside A Levels, and made the school co-educational. The difference was the speed with which he did it. 'Traditionally heads will say, we are going to go co-ed in four years' time, or they'll ask parents and send out questionnaires. I didn't do any of that,' says Seldon, 'because once you consult too widely you get pros and antis and it becomes much more divisive and polarized. So I simply said that we were going to do this. I arrived in January 2006 and two months later, in March, I said that we were going to go co-ed, not in four years' time but in four months' time.'

Needless to say, there were a few casualties along the way. Gideon Heugh, one of the students in the Sixth Form at the time, recalls, 'My house became a girls' house, so we had to vacate our home for it to be refurbished. They added en-suite bathrooms for the girls, which made us a bit resentful. Also there was a strong sense of home – of family and community – among the 50 boys who lived together, and it felt all torn up. We felt there should have been more ceremony around it, but we were just sent an email in the summer holidays. It put a bit of a downer on our last year, probably made us a bit more rebellious. We saw ourselves as being like Harrow, Radley or Tonbridge, a more traditional boys' school, and were resistant to any sort of change.' But more than a decade on and father of a newborn baby girl, he says, 'looking back, it was a bit ridiculous that we were so resistant to change, I think it's great that Seldon turned it around, I'd send my daughter there – if I could afford it.'

This is illustration perhaps that Anthony Seldon was famed for being strategic on the big picture stuff but not so interested in the back-office detail – something Sir Tim Brighouse said of himself, incidentally. And understandably so, considering their workload.

Another point of agreement was the need to have the right people – in this case, the right teachers. After all, a school's core purpose is to educate young people, and if a teacher doesn't uphold this belief then it's difficult to justify their being in the job. We all know teachers who have inspired, and others who have successfully killed a subject we might otherwise have loved.

But, says Seldon, 'Any head will tell you that this is very difficult. Teachers all know who are the weak and the lazy and the malign, and they all grumble endlessly about them, but as soon as the head starts doing anything about it, they get right behind poor old Joe and Sarah who are being bullied.'

Echoing Brighouse's words, Seldon adds, 'The fact is that many staff can and will improve with help and support. Maybe they haven't been valued; maybe it's a problem of motivation or a problem of knowledge or a problem of feeling alienated. We had a constant drive for improving performance. But where it was clear that somebody just didn't want to improve, or they didn't accept that they weren't making the mark with the students, then my view was that it wasn't right or fair for the students – it wouldn't be in any school.' So yes, the school wasn't doing well on numbers when Seldon arrived and he made a few redundancies.

'We had a brilliant team,' says Seldon. 'The senior team was hugely supportive, as were the housemistresses – and we had a fantastic governing body.' With regards to going co-ed, 'The perception was that the school was rather rugger, male, a bit boorish – there had been a reputation of bullying and spiked drinks. So it did take a little bit of persuasion that girls should join.'

But this he did, targeting the daughters of old Wellingtonians first, and ensuring they offered traditional girls' sports while not allowing the reputation for boys' sports – which had always been strong – to slip. 'Anthony did amazing things with the arts as well,' says Lunnon. 'His interest was English and drama; he directed and produced many, many plays in his career. We brought in scholars who weren't brilliant academically but who were virtuoso violinists. Wellington's orchestra is simply phenomenal. Sport is of national and international class. Anthony made an extraordinary amount of progress in a very short space of time.'

So Wellington College was set on its way to being great again, at super speed. But what about the desired 'distinctiveness'?

Well-being

Seldon explains that in the autumn of 2005, while visiting Wellington to speak to the parents about what he might do as head of their children's school when he joined in January, somebody asked him, 'What did he value most in education?' His answer was that the children should be happy. In response to this, one of the parents in the audience approached him after his talk and asked if he knew anything about a new academic field of happiness, and in particular happiness in education. Seldon didn't, but he made it his business to do so, reading the works of psychologist Professor Martin Seligman, whose life's work challenged the status quo of his profession: rather than focusing on the darker side of the human condition, on depression and human misery, Seligman instead focused on human flourishing and well-being, and the field of positive psychology was born.

'This was one of the biggest *aha!* moments in my life,' says Seldon. Seldon had long battled with anxiety and depression himself, and with a determination to be master of his own life and well-being, he had what he describes a 'believing' approach – an implicit understanding that what we believe about ourselves will happen, or at least have a significant probability of happening – and here, 'at last', says Seldon, 'were psychological imperative aids – university-based – for the beliefs that I had held in a covert way all my life'. Here were evidence-based interventions to help young people develop habits that they can then take through life.

To clarify, Seldon explains that actually it wasn't so much about teaching young people how to be happy; rather it was about giving them the resources to live life better and handle themselves with agility, to cope better with adversity, stress and low periods. It was about resilience and letting people live more naturally inside themselves.

Anthony Seldon's introduction of a well-being programme at Wellington College was utterly aligned with his beliefs – but it was also a magnificent marketing coup. One of the threads that weaves through this book is the importance of communication in implementing strategy. Like it or not, it's crucial – and Seldon understood this. 'Of course you have to communicate all the time,' he says, 'because if you don't set the agenda then other people set it for you. I would always be a macro-broadcaster, looking for opportunities to communicate with the maximum number of people.'

Elements of positive psychology – mindfulness, Carol Dweck's growth mindset and so on – are now, if not quite mainstream, certainly featuring in many schools across the country, but Wellington was ahead of the curve and packaged it a little bit differently. In the spring of 2006, the press picked up on the story of the first school in England to be teaching happiness – and suddenly Wellington College was very much on the map.

'Seldon was an absolute genius at marketing,' says Lunnon, 'passionate and relentless in his messaging.' He travelled widely and spoke all over the world, and yet was apparently ever present on the school campus as well, for staff, parents and children.

Along with the well-being programme, Seldon also introduced the idea of 'eight aptitudes' based on Dr Howard Gardner's theory of multiple intelligences, which differentiates human intelligence into a number of specific 'modalities'. It's making the 'intelligence' point in a different way, Seldon explains. Seldon argues that children must never believe they can't do things – this is a crippling and disabling belief, particularly if a child doesn't conform to the factory norms of intelligence that are so often defined in a left-brain cognitive way.

Dr Howard Gardner famously said, 'Don't ask how intelligent a child is, ask rather, how is a child intelligent?' because every child has different strengths, which should be nurtured. Economists, Seldon argues, latched on to this with their theory of comparative advantage, which argues that countries should play to their strengths. Similarly, a human being that grows from its strengths is more likely to be successful. The 'eight aptitudes' adopted at Wellington were logical, linguistic, personal, social, sporting, cultural, moral and spiritual. 'It provided a good scaffold on which to deliver a holistic education,' adds Lunnon. 'It was a good way to say to school kids that you could excel in a lot of ways, and allowed the kids who weren't straightforward academics to thrive.'

There might well have been criticism that an emphasis on well-being and the eight aptitudes was 'La La land, mushing up education, psychobabble on steroids', as Seldon put it. But the argument was put to rest when the figures were analysed. It generated a buzz, teachers and students worked hard on the core academic subjects too, and all of a sudden there was a waiting list – gold dust for any school. And with a waiting list, the school could afford to become more selective and the results spiralled upwards.

'It's fair to say there was a fair bit of cognitive dissidence around the place,' explains Head of Religious Education and Philosophy, Ian Morris, who was appointed the challenge of taking the principles of positive psychology and translating them into something that worked for young people (and incidentally wrote a wonderful book on the subject, called *Learning to Ride Elephants*). 'There was a tension between well-being and exam results,' he says. 'The messaging we got as staff was that results were the most important thing, and that if we had to make a choice, then academics were the most important. There were very clear targets for A–A* grades at GCSE and A Level.'

The year before Anthony Seldon was appointed as head, Wellington College was in 256th position on *The Sunday Times* A Level league table. Eight years on, it had risen to 21. Had it become a great school? Many regard it as the top co-educational boarding school in England. And distinctive? The well-being programme certainly contributed to that, and arguably the school became softer, more cultured, more civilized, though some might lament the passing of its more masculine heritage of military service and sacrifice. Some old Wellingtonians might also lament the fact that their offspring are no longer guaranteed a place. It once had a reputation for being a school for 'all-rounders', and under Seldon became far more academic – an irony not lost when one reflects upon the sound principles of the 'eight aptitudes'.

But considering the league table climate of the English education system in the 21st century, 'Anthony was right,' concedes Ian Morris. 'The school was in real trouble financially and looking job losses in the face. We needed to get exam results up.' Seldon did this and a whole lot more besides. With the school now under the leadership of Julian Thomas, the eight aptitudes narrative has slipped away, but the well-being programme is still very much embedded. It is surely a measure of Seldon's legacy of success that Julian Thomas had the confidence to follow the likes of Eton, Winchester and St Paul's, and withdraw the school from the league tables, which are increasingly regarded as encouraging 'teaching to the test'. 'It is clear that all schools have to genuinely commit to an education which goes way beyond simply the acquisition of grades C–A*,' says Thomas. 'We have to equip our children with the skills and aptitudes they need to live, thrive and survive in the future. Skills such as critical thinking, problem-solving, independent thinking and learning, leadership and creativity.'

We understand and welcome change because change is learning and that's our business.

From *Essential Pieces: The Jigsaw of a Successful School,*
Professor Sir Tim Brighouse

Hoffer once said, 'In an age of great change the learners inherit the earth, while the learned are beautifully equipped to deal with a world that no longer exists.'

Teachers today understand this. Increasing numbers of young and old people alike can use the Internet to become well informed about any particular topic they choose. What is more, the 'deferential' age has given way to the more disputatious and participative present day.

The teacher is no longer, if she ever was, the sole supplier of information. Rather the teacher is the coach, the developer of pupil skills and competence, as well as the wise and trusted guide on values and where to go for further information. She knows that to learn is to change.

But the present day has brought incessant externally-imposed change from successive central governments. So the successful school sees to it that every member of staff understands some of the essentials of change, so they can welcome it, divert it or resist it as a school community decides. The successful school will have inwardly registered some of the rules of change.

The first lesson concerns complex change, and the following diagram shows what happens when any one of five essential ingredients is absent. Of course, it doesn't explain the dysfunctionality which is created when two or three are absent or when all you've got is a succession of 'action plans' with no vision, skills, resources or incentives. But it's a helpful guide to implementing change.

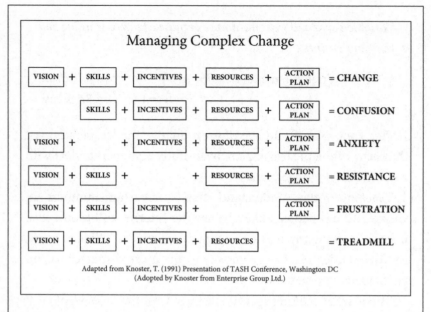

Managing Complex Change

VISION	+	SKILLS	+	INCENTIVES	+	RESOURCES	+	ACTION PLAN	= CHANGE
		SKILLS	+	INCENTIVES	+	RESOURCES	+	ACTION PLAN	= CONFUSION
VISION	+			INCENTIVES	+	RESOURCES	+	ACTION PLAN	= ANXIETY
VISION	+	SKILLS	+			RESOURCES	+	ACTION PLAN	= RESISTANCE
VISION	+	SKILLS	+	INCENTIVES	+			ACTION PLAN	= FRUSTRATION
VISION	+	SKILLS	+	INCENTIVES	+	RESOURCES			= TREADMILL

Adapted from Knoster, T. (1991) Presentation of TASH Conference, Washington DC
(Adopted by Knoster from Enterprise Group Ltd.)

Internally generated change is always welcome. It arises from members of the school community, perhaps in a school improvement group, suggesting change and having it adopted. Externally available change is that sort of change you can embrace and tailor to your needs. This, too, is welcome. Externally mandated change is much more difficult.

Most importantly, welcoming change involves knowing that 'if a thing's worth doing, it's worth doing badly', the first time round during the adoption phase. Of course, the second time round, after review, 'it's worth doing better'. Finally, in the consolidation phase, anything 'is worth doing well'.

References

1. Department for Education statistics
2. Department for Education statistics. Morris, E in conversation with Brighouse, T, Sept 2002
3. ILEA Statistical Report on School Standards, 1990

CHAPTER FIVE

Implementing Strategy in the Arts

The purpose of art is higher than art. What we are really interested in are masterpieces of humanity.

Alonzo King, dancer and choreographer

In times of austerity, do we tighten belts and play cautious, doing the 'same old same old' (maybe just less of it) and wait for the clouds to pass? Or, confident in our excellence and creativity, do we dig deep and take risks not just for survival but to flourish? It takes courage to do the latter – something the Artistic Director and Lead Principal Dancer of English National Ballet, Tamara Rojo, has in spades. Rojo was appointed Artistic Director in 2012, when the country was still reeling from the shock of the 2008 financial crisis and Arts Council funding to English ballet companies was being slashed year on year – there was even talk of cutting the number of ballet companies in the country. Other than a working studio and offices tucked away in a cobbled mews behind the Albert Hall, English National Ballet – a touring company with a remit to deliver ballet to the regions – had no assets, making it particularly vulnerable in such a climate (unlike The Royal Ballet with its Royal Opera House).

A number of visionary directors had come through English National Ballet over the years, defeated by the traditional cautiousness of the board of directors. But this appointment was different. From the start, Tamara Rojo made both her vision and what she needed in order to implement it very clear. She made it a condition of her appointment that she would bring her artistic team with her. The four lead ballet masters at English National Ballet would have to go; in her view they were too traditionalist and it would be impossible to implement her strategy with a team that didn't believe in what she wanted to do. In their place, she appointed ballet masters and mistresses personally hand-picked from around the globe: 72-year-old Loipa Araújo from Cuba as Associate Artistic Director, for her technique and wealth of teaching experience; Yohei Sasaki from Japan; Antonio Castilla from Spain; and Hua Fang Zhang from China. Together, these four would introduce English National Ballet to many different and new styles. It was clear things were going to be very different from this point on.

Early career

Tamara Rojo has a number of winning characteristics, of which perhaps the most obvious are a fierce independence of thought and a determination to excel, shaped by her upbringing and well-honed in her career as a ballerina. Tamara is an only child, born in 1974 to Spanish parents in Canada, where her father was fleeing from Franco's dictatorship and her mother was studying. They returned to Madrid with Tamara as a tiny baby, where her parents are said to have kept an illegal printing press under her cot. Her father described himself as 'an anarchist republican' and she grew up on a diet of hard-hitting political films and demonstrations – and also a belief in possibility.

Aged five, she happened to glimpse a ballet class after school and was hooked. Her parents were neither dancers nor well-off, but supported her through ballet school, studying under the extraordinary Víctor Ullate, on the condition she completed an academic education as well. She did this by attending evening classes after studio rehearsals every day. At 16, she joined Víctor Ullate's dance company in Spain and, in 1994, won a prestigious Gold Medal at a dance competition in Paris that led to an invitation to join Scottish Ballet. Here she spent six months before being approached by Derek Deane, then director of English National Ballet, who quickly promoted her to principal of his company.

Her dancing is astonishing. In 1997, she was named 'Dance Revelation of the Year' for her performance as Clara in *The Nutcracker*, and three years later was invited to become principal dancer at The Royal Ballet, where she danced for 12 years. Tamara says of herself that she wasn't especially gifted, she just worked extraordinarily hard – and pushed through the pain. She famously leapt at the chance to stand in for an injured Darcey Bussell in *Giselle*, despite a sprained ankle of her own, and on another occasion started shaking on stage and carried on dancing regardless until the end of the show, only to discover she had a burst appendix. She has been repeatedly recognized for her artistic excellence with a list of international awards too long to record here, and somewhere along the line squeezed in the time to gain a PhD in performing arts as well. Her thesis was 'Psychological Profile of the Elite Dancer – Vocational Characteristics of the Professional Dancer,' which we can assume is something she knows quite a lot about.

Rojo's application for the job of artistic director at English National Ballet wasn't her first foray into directing a company. While at The Royal Ballet, Spain's government approached her with an idea to set up a touring ballet company in Spain (much like English National Ballet), and she realized it was something that appealed to her. She later participated in training for artistic directors at The National Ballet of Canada, and was a front-runner for the directorship of The Royal Ballet in 2011. But the post for artistic director at English National Ballet came at the right time for her, and it was the right dance company for her too.

Making an impact by being an outsider

'I had been a dancer there for three years,' she says. 'I fell in love with the vision, with the travelling, getting to know the country, but also meeting audiences for which a show is extraordinarily important because it is only once a year.' She's keen to impress that ballet needn't be exclusive, that there are tickets for £10, less than for football or the cinema. English National Ballet was also first to do outreach, to work with schools and bring children into the ballet, to do master classes and collaborations.

Importantly, Rojo also understood that she could make an impact at English National Ballet in a way that would have been much more difficult at The Royal Ballet, say, or The Paris Opera Ballet – companies steeped in absolutes and tradition. 'It's important to understand *where* you can get things done; there are other jobs that might look more attractive – better pay, nice office, whatever – but you can't *do* anything.' English National Ballet was vulnerable, but also adaptable – and Rojo's vision was to create an identity for English National Ballet that was uniquely its own.

As suggested by her insistence on appointing a new team of ballet masters that brought with them expertise in different dance styles from around the globe, Tamara Rojo's artistic vision was to renew the art form. It was to honour the classical repertoire but perform it in a novel and different way, to bring in collaborators in the form of composers, designers, choreographers and dancers from all over the world – and to emotionally engage audiences of today. To be radical and take risks.

When asked if she had any alternative course of action in the event that this approach might fail, she answers, 'Not really, because the question was, does the UK need so many ballet companies? We needed to say quickly that we're different, we're doing something extraordinary, we have our own identity and our own reason to exist – we are going to become the groundbreaking company, the risk-taking company, the company that does things outside the box. Nobody else is doing this so you need to keep us. It was the only way I felt we could answer that question.'

Rojo recognizes that the unique quality she brings to English National Ballet is an outside perspective. 'I didn't come from a traditional ballet school,' she says. 'I came from a small school in Spain that had a very short history – no tradition to take care of.' Her teacher, Víctor Ullate, came from a folkloric training before joining Maurice Béjart's

Ballet; he had excellent classical technique but wasn't constrained by tradition. 'He would teach us the skeleton of classical technique,' says Rojo, 'and then every week or two, we would change styles. Sometimes we would do things in a Bournonville Danish tradition, other times he wanted us to try a more Bolshoi Russian tradition, other times he was more into the French Academy, other times he would make us learn the repertoire of The Royal Ballet, but we felt that all the choices were valid and the point was to be good at as many as possible – that would make a great artist.'

It came as something of a surprise to Rojo as a dancer at English National Ballet, and then The Royal Ballet, that there was considered to be a 'correct' way of doing things, because this was the way things had always been done. 'I thought that artists were here to question the status quo, to create – not just to repeat or to imitate – but to bring something of their own. I was consistently told that I had to look like somebody else, I had to dance like somebody else that had come before me – and I was *dead*,' she says with emphasis.

If not wholly complimentary about the traditionalist approach to dance at English National Ballet, she was very much in favour of its recruiting process and the fact she had to present her vision and a plan to the board of directors – all non-executive, and most with long, successful careers in financial services or law. 'I would recommend businesses to do that,' she says. 'Get the last three people for the executive role to actually present a vision for the company – for their own good – because they have to really dig into the business, and say, this is what it is, this is where I'm taking it to and this is how I'm going to do it.' She also valued that she had a full six months from the day she was offered the job to the day she started work.

Focusing on the role

But how, one wonders, does she manage to juggle her time between her twin roles as Principal Dancer and Artistic Director? The answer is that it is shifting; as time marches on she is dedicating more of her time to directing the company and less to dance – the ratio is now about 9:1. Something she embraces, holding the view that a director can have a wider impact on society than a dancer.

And what about focus of the mind? In an age of increasing distractions and mobile devices within arm's reach of school children and chief execs alike, the issue of focusing on important work is a universal problem. In efforts to calm the mind and focus, traditions of the East – meditation, mindfulness and yoga – are no longer the preserve of the countercultural but have become mainstream. The concept of 'flow' or being in the zone – the mental state in which a person performing an activity is fully immersed in a feeling of energized focus – is commonly realized in dance, as in music and different forms of sport and art. But is it transferable to the office?

'It is something I continuously struggle with,' says Rojo, referring to the constant movement of people and non-stop questioning both from her emails and those physically present in the office. 'For me, ballet class was always like a small meditation. It was an abstraction – you could focus on very specific [movements] of your body, so your mind was not wandering. I only realized that I was losing focus when I stopped doing class every day,' she continues. She wasn't getting more done – despite longer hours in the office she was actually less efficient, 'because my mind hadn't quite brought itself together'.

'So I set some rules very early on,' she says. She reinstated her daily routine of an hour's dance class every morning and said that 'unless the world was falling apart no one would come to class with questions for me as artistic director. It is a meditation and because my mind is at rest I have the best ideas. I have a notebook next to me at the barre and I just write them down, and that works for me.'

She has also recently established a habit of removing herself from the office and working at home for four or five hours twice a week, 'to have space – space to read, listen to music, watch videos from choreographers who send me things, space to think about collaborations and search for designers, space to even browse Instagram to see what other people are doing and where the ballet world is going. You can't quite do that in the office. There is a perception that you are wasting your time because you're not answering email. But I have a creative duty to come up with ideas as well as solve issues in the office.'

Artistic vision

And indeed, it is for her artistic vision that she has been universally applauded. She invited choreographer Akram Khan to create a piece of work to commemorate the First World War. His blending of contemporary and classical ballet with Kathak dance delivered such an emotional impact that she asked him to look at the oldest romantic ballet in history, *Giselle*, in which he reimagined Giselle as a 21st century refugee. The ballet was filmed and shown in 140 cinemas worldwide. Within just two years of Rojo's directorship, English National Ballet had taken all 67 dancers to perform for the first time in history at the Palais Garnier in Paris, with a new production of the most famous ballet in its repertoire, *Le Corsaire*.

'I knew that the company would change fast,' says Rojo, 'because it's lean – but in fact it changed faster than I thought. There were moments like Paris when I thought, OK so we are already here, have I thought ahead enough? Do I have the next challenge? Or do I actually have to pause a little bit, give time for the organization to breathe?'

That same year English National Ballet performed a new initiative called 'She Said': a programme of all-women choreography. This arose from Rojo's personal experience as a ballerina; in 20 years, she hadn't once worked with a director who had commissioned a female choreographer. 'I felt there was something lacking,' says Rojo. 'There are a lot of things that I felt – that I'm sure all the women felt – that we were not expressing on stage, that nobody was seeing. It was constantly quite a sexualized conversation, if not objectified, sometimes. I thought we needed the other side of this conversation.' Rojo actively sought female choreographers, and the resulting expansion of the company's repertoire with the triple-bill She Said programme (with choreographers Annabelle Lopez Ochoa, Aszure Barton and Yabin Wang), together with Akram Khan's *Giselle*, won English National Ballet the prized 2017 Olivier Award for Outstanding Achievement in Dance.

There is no question that Tamara Rojo has had a startling impact on English National Ballet – all while Arts Council subsidies have fallen in percentage terms from 47 per cent to 33 per cent during her tenure. 'It is very difficult to convince somebody to give you money for a production you've been doing for 30 years,' she explains, 'but if you have something new and exciting to offer, that attracts investors. Then, by doing exciting things, people want to come and see it – and the international arena starts to pay attention and we get more international tours, which bring in a lot of money. It's a virtuous circle.'

The decision-making process is one that lies with the executive team (Tamara Rojo as artistic director and Patrick Harrison as executive director), but every decision has to be approved by the board of directors – which, like the majority of charitable boards, is risk-averse. 'Sometimes it is quite difficult,' explains Rojo, 'because for boards it very often comes down narrowly to numbers and they don't completely understand the relationship of risk-taking.' Though, she adds, 'they do better now, because I've proved it'.

Communication/facilitating change

Communication is a crucial element of executing any strategy. While successfully persuading the board of directors, how does Rojo cascade her vision through the dance company to those who deliver the performances – the dancers? 'Talking, talking, talking,' she says. 'When you think you've explained it ten times, explain it ten other times. In my head the path is crystal clear; the objective is like a light, I can see it. But that doesn't mean that everyone else can, and it doesn't mean that I am explaining it clearly enough. People hear things and they interpret it in their own personal way. So you think you have said something and they go away and they do something completely different.' In addition, some members of staff have been with the company from the beginning of its transformation but others have joined later, so the only way it works for Rojo is to constantly remind people – at every meeting, every decision – where their journey started, where they are now, and where they are going in the future.

Rojo meets with the dancers every Friday; they sit together and discuss plans for the following year, or the marketing campaign. Directors of the board and staff from different functions of the company – outreach, development, marketing, finance, HR and music – are invited along to share views on their objectives so that the dancers can contextualize their part in the whole and make their contributions as well.

Since Rojo brought in new choreographers – many from contemporary dance – the creation of new work in the studio tends to be collaborative, with the dancers having a voice. Often a choreographer will outline the story and the characters, then ask the dancers to go away and create something and come back in an hour or so to work on it together. Which as Rojo explains is actually one of the problems for her as artistic director; it is 'very counterintuitive to a dancer who has been trained in a classical ballet school'.

Rojo describes how this shift in mindset was 'one of the hardest things – not so much for the younger dancers, but for the ballerinas who have been here for a long period of time, where they have consistently been told there is only one way of doing things, and they have been doing it for 15 or 20 years, thinking this is the right way to do it.' But Rojo was telling them, 'there is no such thing, and not only is there no such thing but I can't let you do it like this anymore, I have to ask you to do it differently'. There was, she admits, a lot of shock and tears.

It was an issue Rojo had anticipated. 'I wanted to keep the dancers because I felt it was unfair on them that they had come here with [another] director. I wanted to work with the people that were here, and see if they could adapt to the new way, so I didn't fire anybody. But slowly during the six years, sometimes little, sometimes bigger groups have changed – but that has been more organic.'

Moving to new headquarters

Another massive change that Rojo has overseen is a move from the company's charming but small house in South Kensington to a shiny, purpose-built £37m building in London City Island, in 2019. The move was part necessity – the old property was clearly short on space – and partly an opportunity to further expand the work of English National Ballet.

For the first time in 20 years, English National Ballet is now under the same roof as English National Ballet School: a specialist ballet school for students aged 16 to 19 years old. The new building, at 93,000 square feet, is four times the size of the old buildings combined and includes a theatre with fly-tower and full rig where they can rehearse productions with full technical support before they tour – something they used only to be able to do by renting a theatre at a cost of around £50,000 a week. The new premises allow English National Ballet to create more work, develop and nurture talent, and reach a large audience by enabling and creating more performances – and importantly to be more resilient, with a more enterprising business model for both the company and the school.

Rojo's story at English National Ballet is one of dedication, grit and huge accomplishment, with ambitions still for the future. It is, she says, 'about creating a company that has meaning and impact and purpose for this society for which we owe it to, because we live off their taxes'. And is there anything she would change? 'I would love to be able to celebrate achievement more often rather than worry about the next thing,' she reflects. 'I think it's important.'

CHAPTER SIX

Employing Artificial Intelligence to Implement a Strategy for Sustainable Energy

AI isn't just infiltrating everyday life, it's going to transform entire industries.

Bernard Marr, futurist, author and strategic business and
technology advisor, *Forbes* magazine 2020

The idea of an artificial intelligence of sorts isn't new – the first accounts of automata are in Homer's *Iliad*, in approximately 800 BC – and through the centuries these ideas have developed into the more familiar ideas of robots, cybernetics and now artificial intelligence (AI). It was mathematician and theoretical computer scientist Alan Turing (who famously cracked the German's 'Enigma' code) who began to grapple with the notion of a machine-based intelligence in the 1940s – and in the 1950s, posed the question now known as the Turing test: can machines think? The idea being that a machine could be presumed to think if it exhibits intelligence which a human being might consider human.

Today, the use of artificial intelligence is growing and spreading through society. (Here we're defining artificial intelligence as the theory and development of computer systems able to perform tasks normally requiring human intelligence, such as visual perception, speech recognition and decision-making; and more specifically we're talking about machine learning – a form of AI where computer systems learn for themselves from examples, data and experience.) As machines make decisions on our behalf and perform jobs that we might otherwise do (and often better than we could), it's no wonder there might be a degree of apprehension and even fear surrounding these developments.

Vivienne Ming, a theoretical neuroscientist and AI specialist, is of the view that what we really need to be worrying about is not only AI-related labour market disruption for factory workers, but for 'brainworkers' too. She believes that the global professional middle class is about to be blindsided. And to support her view, she cites a recent competition at Columbia University between human lawyers and their artificial counterparts, in which both read a series of non-disclosure agreements with loopholes in them. The AI found 95 per cent of them, and the humans just 88 per cent. But here's the real differentiator: the humans took 90 minutes to read them while AI took only 22 seconds. Game, set and match to AI.

While we can only speculate at the speed and the depth with which AI will infiltrate our daily and working lives, there's one thing not in doubt: AI is here to stay. Once invented, it can't be un-invented, and if one company chooses not to adopt the advantages it can offer, then another will – and the first will struggle to stay in business.

The story in this chapter is about a long-established oil and gas company that has pioneered the use of revolutionary engineering and technical equipment to extract carbon from some of the most challenging environments in the world, and yet – apart from two young employees – it was remarkably slow to see emerging developments in the digital space. These two young employees, Jens Festervoll and Stein Petter Aannerud, used their combined wit and persuasive powers to form a small, innovative group within the company, and in doing so they played a part in steering the company toward a more efficient, profitable and environmentally sustainable future.

The company in question is Equinor, the Norwegian multinational energy company. Through the years, Equinor's strong focus on sustainability has earned it worldwide recognition that is unusual in the oil and gas industry. In 2014, it was ranked the fourth most sustainable corporation in the world, regardless of industry, and in 2016, it was recognized by CDP as the world's most sustainable oil and gas producer. Still, it acknowledges that there is much work to be done; its strategy is to produce oil and gas more effectively with lower greenhouse gas emissions, to be a leader within carbon capture and storage, and to invest substantially in renewable energy.

Jens Festervoll, senior adviser of corporate innovation, global strategy and business development, explains: 'Our ambition is to increase investment level toward renewable energy to between 15 and 20 per cent capital expenditure in 2030, compared with around 1 per cent today.' While cautioning that there are many variables that might make this more aspirational than absolute, he acknowledges this is 'a significant step up by our executives' and, in his view, would be utterly impossible without the use of digital technologies. 'Digitalization enables the company to work differently, think differently, act differently,' he stresses. 'It enables the company to get things done more efficiently in a cost-effective way.' Big picture? Digitalization is a critical enabler in reducing greenhouse gas emissions.

Getting Equinor interested in digitalization

Nonetheless, Jens Festervoll's efforts to navigate the corporate structure in order to put digitalization on the agenda have met with a fair bit of resistance along the way. Until recently, Festervoll was head of corporate strategy and, in the autumn of 2014 was responsible for the organization of an off-site meeting with the executive management team in which they looked at five global 'megatrends' – climate change, digital transformation, demographic change, urbanization and globalization. From these five megatrends, the executive management team was to pick one important subject to discuss. To Festervoll's surprise and frustration, the subject chosen was demographics, not digital transformation. It took another year for Festervoll to persuade the CEO that digital transformation was the more important subject, if not *the* most important subject – and still there was resistance. The CEO said it was too early to put the subject of digitalization to the board of directors; first there needed to be a greater maturity and understanding of the subject.

So Jens Festervoll and his corporate strategy team tried a different tack. Their belief was that to accelerate the digital agenda they would need to both educate executives and engage the workforce. One of the tasks within their brief was to organize leadership training programmes, working closely with the HR department. So they put together a training programme for a dozen senior leaders that naturally included how to manage teams, how to delegate and so on, but in addition they slipped in an important element on the big issue of digitalization. The senior leaders were assigned a project titled 'Taking Statoil [now Equinor] beyond 2025 Digitalization', in which they were invited to talk to people within the organization and collate views on what a world with digitalization might look like in a decade's time, then come back with recommendations on where to take digitalization within the organization. In April 2017, the senior leaders did just that, and their recommendation was to set up a Centre of Digital Excellence.

Essentially, Festervoll and his team had created a movement using the internal network to create leverage. 'We had no clear mandate, vision or goal,' says Festervoll, 'but by the end of June so many people were talking about it that the company had to do something about it.' In August 2017, Equinor put its vast industrial strength behind digitalization and committed 1 to 2 billion NOK to creating a Centre of Digital Excellence by 2020 – this was on top of existing investments in IT.

'We were given the opportunity to prove ourselves,' says Festervoll. 'It was clear the business needed to bring money to the table. It's not rocket science, it's still just hard work – if you don't use the people within the organization then nothing will happen.' A chief digital officer was tasked with setting up the Digital Centre of Excellence, at

Sandsli in Bergen on the west coast, and Festervoll left his previous role to help him set it up. The primary objective of this centre of excellence was to drive the development of digital solutions in a way that was both innovative and included all disciplines; the overall aim, to make Equinor better equipped to move forward as a broad energy company – not just an oil and gas company but a renewable energy company as well.

Robotic Processing Automation

One of the key areas of development was RPA, Robotic Processing Automation, and the man appointed to be in charge of RPA, Stein Petter Aannerud, was an economist by training and passionate about the efficiencies this technology could bring about. 'The concept had already been proven in banking and insurance, so we knew it worked – there was a lot of low-lying fruit,' says Aannerud, 'but this was new technology and nobody at Equinor knew anything about it. Equinor is a big bureaucratic organization. We knew that if we were to do this quickly, we were to do it differently, so without asking too much mandate, we started playing about with ideas.'

The first task was to establish whether or not there was a need. 'Most of the journey that we have done with RPA has been business driven,' says Festervoll. 'People are pressured on margins, on capacity, on speed – and are really curious to see what technology can do to help their part of the business. I think this is one of our success criteria. I hear that elsewhere there can be a lot of resistance to technology when you try to push it, but we managed to create a "pull" in the organization by providing people with information and pointing out what RPA could do for them.'

Now might be the point to outline what RPA actually is and does. For the uninitiated (like me) it is not a physical robot as its name suggests; rather it is a software robot which can be designed to do specific tasks on our behalf. We are used to automation software that works within systems, but this new generation works *between* systems, so information received on a PDF attached to an email can be automatically transferred on to an Excel spreadsheet or a database, for example. It mimics the way a human being would do it but much faster, and without mistakes – saving a phenomenal amount of time. It can work 365 days a year with no breaks, no lunches and no holidays. So instead of starting the day (and likely half the morning) manually punching numbers from a PDF into an Excel spreadsheet, you can get straight down to the interesting bit of analysing the data. 'We're not replacing humans with robots, but merely taking the robot out of the human – namely, the boring stuff,' says Aannerud.

So having established a need, how did they implement RPA within the organization? Naturally they employed a consultant with experience in the speciality, but essentially 'we just got on and did it', says Aannerud. 'There is no room for failure at the sharp end of the oil and gas industry,' he says, 'but at the back end – in the office – there should be, but people are afraid to do anything new because of the safety culture that permeates throughout the organization. It shouldn't matter in the office – don't be afraid, be more disruptive! The only downside is failure, but then at least you have learned something along the way.'

'One of the first questions we had was how do we give robots access to data?' says Aannerud. They didn't have an answer at first, but then with a bit of lateral thinking they realized that when a new employee is hired to the company, he or she applies for and is granted access to a particular data system they are working on, so why not adopt the same approach for software robots? Thus, software robots adopted the name 'virtual workers', which indeed they are. 'Our first virtual worker was Robert Robot and we employed him as part of an agreement with recruitment,' says Aannerud with a smile. Then someone required a software robot to perform another specific task and 'we employed Roberta Robot, Robert's wife!' At this point somebody apparently woke up to what was going on: *You can't employ virtual workers in the company!* 'But by doing it the way we did we saved a lot of time,' says Aannerud, and it was successful too. An agreement was made with the recruiting department that alongside permanent employees and consultants, there would be a third employment category of virtual employees. 'When you don't know who to ask, just move forward,' says Aannerud.

'It was all about networks as well,' he adds, 'and stepping on a few toes – but hopefully the right ones. The non-threatening approach, doing it with a smile, was helpful. It also helped not being a techie guy, because I could push the business case as being the most important, with technology just as an enabler.'

The company employed 50 software robots – each for a different task and each with its own identity number (or name, in the case of Rob and Roberta) – in the first nine months, saving an estimated 50,000 hours per year – a number that has grown quickly to approximately 400,000 hours per year. 'This is a fairly large number in a company like ours,' says Aannerud. There are now software robots operating all over the company and 'those who have been transformed – seen the light, so to speak – are fully behind it', says Aannerud.

Benefits and challenges

One very happy customer said that it's about streamlining and being more efficient, freeing her from repetitive tasks and releasing more time to be creative, to challenge herself and pursue innovation. Another employee recognized the need for the company to automate processes and took the trouble to teach himself programming in his spare time. His first automation program simplified the task of informing people when equipment was ready to pick up from factories; his software robot checks for new document numbers, prepares an email and sends this along with a receipt to inform people that their equipment is ready, saving a huge amount of time and improving accuracy.

This technology isn't revolutionary – it's essentially the same as that used when you or I buy a product on line and are informed by email when it is dispatched from the warehouse and what time to expect the delivery at your front door. 'The difference,' points out Stein Petter Aannerud, 'is the scale of operation.' In an organization the size of Equinor, present in more than 30 countries around the world, there are tens of thousands of shipments being dispatched to hundreds of sites every hour of the day. Before RPA, the task of keeping track of all these shipments was too vast to contemplate; too complex for humans to get their heads round. But with RPA, the impossible becomes possible, and the potential uplift in the efficiency of supply chain logistics makes the bottom-line figures very attractive.

But not everyone in the company embraces RPA in the same way. 'If you read the papers, there are a lot of negative articles around robotics,' says Aannerud. 'One of my jobs has been to demystify this a bit – and also tell the good stories. But we need to acknowledge there are people who feel they are outdated and won't be capable of working in a digital Equinor. We acknowledge their concerns while letting them know there can be a future for them; they need to learn a few new tricks and techniques and there will be a job for them in the company.'

Essentially it comes down to information, communication and the appropriate training. Classroom training on RPA is offered and some 500 people have taken up the chance to learn – far more than are actually using the technology. 'When people start to understand the upside, then they can see the opportunities and the ball starts rolling,' says Aannerud.

Clearly their approach of being business-led – of educating staff and employing RPA where it can best inject efficiencies – has produced results. A Forrester Report from 2018 that looked at the adoption of RPA across every business sector worldwide rated Equinor in the top 1 per cent of the world in terms of maturity in using this technology. 'I was a bit surprised,' says Jens Festervoll, 'but we are on a really steep curve of implementation, we're moving quite rapidly, and I have yet to hear of anybody moving faster than us in this area.'

'We also believe the data will be crucial for us to drive the business forward,' says Festervoll. He qualifies, 'There is no intelligence in RPA.

It is rule-based; the robot does what it's been programmed to do within the rules that you've set or constraints that you've given it – but what it does give us, over time, is great data quality in all the processes that the robot has run that can then be analysed.' Equinor's operations generate huge quantities of data – more than 26 petabytes are stored in Equinor's databases, equivalent to 50 times the US gene database – and this could be set to double every other year. Moving forward, advanced analysis of this data, as well as machine learning, will aid optimal decision-making across the company, from where to explore new resources, to how to enhance recovery from reservoirs, to how best to optimize trading. 'What we have done is a very natural and important first step to get us going on this journey,' he says.

In January 2019, in a very clear demonstration of Equinor's commitment to digitalization, it formally opened two digital support centres in Bergen: the Integrated Operations Centre (IOC) and the Geo Operations Centre (GOC). The centres ensure quicker and better decisions through close interaction with offshore operations, and have four key objectives: to streamline production, reduce and ideally prevent downtime, reinforce safety and reduce greenhouse gas emissions.

One of the best examples to illustrate how Equinor now works with digitalization is what they call a 'digital twin', essentially a virtual copy of a physical oilfield on a computer screen, enabled by the employment of a comprehensive network of thousands upon thousands of sensors. It is technology also being used in organizations such as NASA and Formula One, and allows them to have a constant overview of what is happening.

The applications of such sensor technology are numerous. A geoscientist at the Geo Operations Centre explains that they receive huge volumes of data when they drill. Sensors on the drilling equipment, deep underground, mean they can tell in what kind of rock they are drilling and whether or not there is water, oil or gas. The job of the geoscientists is then to guide the drilling in the best way possible, based on the information they get in.

From her desk onshore, a process engineer has access to vast volumes of data showing temperatures, pressure and vibrations on the majority of critical equipment on the platforms. Numbers, graphs and drawing cover her screen. She explains that the people in the control room on the platforms monitor everything all the time, but whereas they effectively have their broad beams on, she can have her high beams on, and look a little further for trends and developments to find ways to optimize the system.

One of the most obvious cost savings offered by sensor technology is in the maintenance of offshore rigs. In the energy industry, as in many other engineering operations as well, health and safety are naturally enough at the top of the agenda. It would always have been beneficial to be able to track the wear and tear of component parts, but so stringent are the health and safety measures around the risk of fire that a 'human' monitor wouldn't be permitted to take photographs of component parts with a mobile phone, for instance; rather he or she would have to record observational notes with a pencil and notepad. Consequently, it didn't happen. Instead, component parts of an operating station were – and largely still are – maintained and replaced on a calendar basis, usually one that allows a comfortable safety margin, rather than on need. Clearly not all components wear down at the same rate so this blanket approach means that many components are replaced when actually they still have quite a run of life in them. Sensor technology turns this process on its head. Rather than replacing components according to the calendar, it allows the replacement of components according to need – with enormous uplifts in efficiency and cost savings, while also of course affording the added environmental benefit of a reduction in material waste.

To date Equinor has implemented this sensor technology for maintenance on the Johan Sverdrup oilfield in just one small part of the offshore rig jigsaw puzzle: valves, clearly a vital part of any piping system. It has already generated significant cost savings, and for further benefits, all that is needed is to roll out the technology across all component parts and all its platforms.

Then, the next step is to create a digital catalogue of all component parts and 3D-print them to demand. This is a principle already applied in a number of industries. Think of publishing. There was a time when, as an author, I might order a couple of thousand books from the publisher and fill my spare room to overloading and sell them in small clusters at conferences and events. Today, I can ring up and order 20 or 30 printed to demand, or even two or three if it suits. It's fantastically convenient and, importantly, gives me back my spare room and ensures I don't have unsold books gathering mould. Transfer this principle into the energy business and the cost savings are massive. Invariably, oil and gas rigs are positioned in remote and difficult environments, which means that companies stockpile costly spare part inventories for backup in case of unscheduled maintenance or downtime. Much of this spare part inventory never sees the light of day. Digital cataloguing and 3D printing does away with this completely. And, says Stein Petter Aannerud, 'a pilot is already up and running'.

And in time, the idea is that the process will be taken a step further: there will be notification that a part needs replacing, followed up by an order for it to be 3D printed. Then it will be sent out to the field by drone, and finally installed by a robot (a physical robot this time). It is thought this fully automated process will be feasible in a few years. The technology already exists, all that's needed is a commitment to go for it.

Great news for the organization in terms of safety, efficiency and cost saving – but maybe not quite such good news if you are a technician working on the rigs. Aannerud acknowledges that jobs might be lost, but not yet. 'I think it's a bit exaggerated how many people will lose their jobs; it will take longer than we think. By 2030, if we do nothing, half the company would have retired,' he says, 'do we recruit to replace people doing tedious work, or recruit people doing more productive forward-leaning activities? Things are changing so the question is, how can I as a person start manoeuvring myself for the future?'

'Jens and I have been part of a really interesting journey over the past two years,' he concludes. 'It's been really fun...and extremely frustrating. A lot of digitalization is quite simple and down to earth. It saves time, materials and money,' he says. 'The resistance isn't the technology but the people, they are happy to do things the way they have been done for ever and it's hard to persuade people to do things differently. It's like two steps forwards, four steps backwards, five steps sideways. You need more than one individual to deal with the frustration; we can get really annoyed by the lack of understanding of the importance of doing this – but when you succeed,' he says, 'it's a huge victory to turn people around.'

It isn't just the odd person that Aannerud and Festervoll has turned around, though. They have been instrumental in creating a movement that has turned around a significant part of an organization – a vast, bureaucratic organization at that, with over 20,000 employees that harnesses energy in more than 30 countries worldwide. Of the ten fossil fuel giants, it is Equinor that is projected to invest most in wind and solar over the next five years, by quite some margin – about $10billion, equivalent to 57 per cent of the $17.5 billion combined spend of all ten. Equinor has also signed a Memorandum of Understanding with Shell to collaborate on digital solutions, to exchange expertise in areas such as data science, artificial intelligence and 3D printing. The two companies have already collaborated closely in the Open Subsurface Data Universe (OSDU) initiative and see many mutual benefits as they both have cloud-based digital solutions as an approach to their industry's digital transformation. Equinor will be grateful – as will Shell, and the wider world – for Aannerud's and Festervoll's combined energy and foresight in adopting digital technology that's there for the taking, that will improve efficiency and take a step closer towards a sustainable energy supply for the future. Not bad for a project that started its life as a research exercise in a leadership development programme.

CHAPTER SEVEN

The Power of Mindset in Making Things Happen

Whatever you can do or dream you can, begin it. Boldness has genius, power and magic in it. Begin it now.

Johann Wolfgang von Goethe, poet, playwright, novelist, scientist, and statesman.

It was in the spring of 1921 that Cheshire-born mountaineer George Mallory walked across the Tibetan plateau as a member of the first Mount Everest reconnaissance expedition, and in the hundred years since, mountaineering in the Himalayas and Karakoram has largely been dominated by western climbers. In these two highest mountain ranges in the world, there are 14 'eight-thousanders' – mountains that stand more than 8,000 metres in height above sea level with their summits in the 'Death Zone', where reduced levels of oxygen mean that people die simply because they have climbed too high. Each of the 14 eight-thousanders was first climbed in the golden age of Himalayan climbing between the years 1950 and 1964. In 1986, the celebrated Italian mountaineer, Reinhold Messner, was the first to climb the collection of all 14 eight-thousanders – remarkably, without the use of supplementary oxygen. And since then, some 40 climbers have followed suit; some (like Messner) climbing without supplementary oxygen, some forging new routes, some climbing in the winter, but none in a timeframe of less than a little under eight years.

Whilst these achievements are extraordinary and represent the best of the exploratory and pioneering spirit of mankind, those who have dug a little deeper into the history books will know that, with the odd exception, none of these mountaineering feats would have been accomplished without the tireless support of the tough mountain people of the local communities. On the very first Everest expedition in 1921, the British team gathered Sherpas[1], Bhutias[2] and porters in Darjeeling before making the 300-mile march in the quest to find an approach to climb Everest. In 1953, when a British expedition put the first two men, Edmund Hillary and Sherpa Tensing Norgay, on the summit, there were 350 porters and 20 Sherpas climbing in support. In 1993, I can say categorically that I would not have stepped foot on Everest without the Sherpas, and certainly I wouldn't have reached the summit without the companionship and moral support of Ang Passang and Kami Tchering. Today, Sherpas continue to play an integral role on Everest expeditions in what is now the commercial era. No Sherpas, no expeditions.

For those who were born and reside in the Himalayas, the mountains are naturally an environment in which they have an advantage over those who visit now and again. The Sherpas are astoundingly strong and fast at altitude, and through the years have quietly been breaking each other's speed records. The fastest official ascent from the base camp to the summit of Everest is by Lhakpa Gelu Sherpa and stands at 10 hours, 56 minutes and 46 seconds, in 2003. And although not an official time record, Pemba Dorje claims to have climbed it the following year in 8 hours and 10 minutes. These are astonishing times when you consider that most of us measure an ascent of Everest in weeks and months, and yet few people are interested beyond their immediate community.

It is wonderfully heart-lifting, then, that on 18 January 2021, news broke that ten Nepalese climbers smashed a climbing record that had eluded elite mountaineers for the best part of 40 years – that to climb K2, the so-called Savage Mountain, in the middle of the winter. At 8,611 metres, K2 is the second highest mountain in the world after Everest, but widely regarded as the most treacherous – and the last of the 14 eight-thousanders to have been climbed in the winter.

Of the ten climbers who stepped in unison onto K2's summit, somehow managing to draw enough breath to sing Nepal's national anthem, one stands out – for two reasons. First, he was the only one of the ten to climb without the benefit of supplementary oxygen, making him the only person in the world ever to have made a winter ascent of K2 without oxygen. And secondly, in 2019, he achieved what many thought to be impossible and climbed all 14 eight-thousand metre peaks in an astonishing six months and six days. His name is Nirmal Purja, better known as Nimsdai. And in the context of executing strategy, he is the embodiment of the power of a positive mindset in the setting and accomplishment of goals.

Soldier turns mountaineer

I first met Nimsdai shortly before he set out on his mission to climb the fourteen eight-thousanders, at an event at the Royal Geographical Society (with IBG) in London, in the spring of 2019. He was virtually unknown in mountaineering circles at that point, and with reason. For the past 16 years, he had served in the British Army – first in the Brigade of Gurkhas and then in the Special Boat Service. He had only just handed in his notice in order to climb this collection of high peaks in his self-appointed timeframe of seven months – a project he called Project Possible. The purpose of the event was to find a sponsor, and I had been invited along to interview and contextualize his accomplishments to date. Quietly behind the scenes it turned out that he had already proved a phenomenal climber at extreme altitude – and yet I'll confess, like many other people, I thought his ambition unachievable. Even if it were logistically possible, which I doubted, it was unfathomable to imagine the strength and recovery speeds required to repeatedly climb into the Death Zone. It was more than 25 years since I had climbed Everest, but I clearly recall the weight loss and exhaustion after the ascent, and the longing to lie on a beach for a very, very long time. And then what of the weather? He would need to be extraordinarily lucky to repeatedly hit favourable weather windows, 14 times in quick succession.

We learned that evening that Nimsdai was born in 1983, one of five children with a sister and three much older brothers. He was born in a village called Dana at some 1,600m elevation, in the Myagdi district of Western Nepal, and at the age of four, he moved with his family to the sub-tropical southern region of Chitwan, better known for one-horned rhinos and Bengal tigers than snowy Himalayan peaks. His mother worked on a farm. 'The work load of caring for a young family while bringing money home through hard labour must have been exhausting,' says Nimsdai, 'but she didn't quit, a lot of my work ethic came from my mother.' His father and two of his older brothers were in the Gurkhas. There was never much money, but his brothers sent home a chunk of their wages so that Nimsdai could be educated at an English-speaking boarding school in Chitwan, where he went from the age of five – and all that Nimsdai ever wanted was to follow them into the Gurkhas. Boarding school suited him, and certainly toughened him up. 'Everybody slept in a hostel, where the older kids held the power and the teachers beat the children if they ever stepped out of line,' he says. 'It was my first challenge, I had to learn how to survive in such a tough environment – and quickly.' He was a natural athlete – a fast runner and kickboxer – but had some health issues along the way. He contracted tuberculosis at the age of 10 and was later diagnosed with asthma, but not once did he allow himself to think that any of these ailments would get in the way of his living life to the full. From a very young age, it seems, he developed an exceptionally positive mindset – a mindset that was to see him study and train hard to pass the notoriously brutal and unforgiving selection for the Gurkhas, and then to reach for his next challenge, which was to join the Special Boat Service. Several Gurkhas had progressed to the SAS, but none to the SBS before Nimsdai. The SBS was different – operators in the squadron had to be able to swim and dive during combat, and Gurkhas came from a landlocked country. Operating in water was a whole new experience for Nimsdai, but he trained hard, swimming 2,500 metres in a single session, and dragging himself from his bed at 2.00am on gloomy English winter nights to carry 75lb loads eight miles or so from Maidstone barracks to Chatham. Nimsdai credits the military for what he calls his 100 per cent philosophy. 'It's simple, works for me. If I give 100 per cent, I can put hand on heart and know I've given everything,' he says, 'can't do more than that.'

Mountains were a relatively late addition to Nimsdai's life. 'The first thing anyone says when you tell them you're a Gurkha, is Everest,' he says. 'They assume you know the mountains, but I hadn't ever been there.' A decade of joking and sniping from fellow soldiers and he'd had enough. In 2012, aged 29, he and a friend headed to Everest and asked a guide to lead them up it. 'It was all a rush, we were getting him to show us how to use crampons³ on grass at Base Camp,' says Nimsdai. He didn't climb Everest that year; instead, he climbed a lesser peak, Louche East, a little way down the valley. Then in quick succession he climbed Aconcagua, the highest mountain in South America, and closer to home, one of the 8,000-metre peaks, Dhaulagiri. What he learned, he says, a little shy to deliver the words, is that he has an 'awesome physiology'. His body acclimatizes extraordinarily well to altitude, and in addition he has the strength and compactness to lean in and bulldoze through any weather. To steal a term from economists (as does Sir Anthony Seldon when talking about countries, and also humans, playing to their strengths), Nimsdai had discovered his 'comparative advantage' at extreme altitude. This, combined with his indomitable spirit, was to prove him unstoppable.

He knows his limits, however. In 2016, on leave from service in Afghanistan and waiting for his next deployment, he had a month for rest and relaxation – just long enough, he thought, to climb Everest. With money from a bank loan that was supposedly to buy a new car, and support from his ever-patient wife, Suchi, he flew to Kathmandu. There wasn't time for the usual acclimatization trek to the base camp to allow the body to adjust to the reduced oxygen levels at altitude – so instead he hitched a ride in a helicopter. Five days into the climb and he felt dreadful; he lay in his sleeping bag, listening to his rattling lungs. 'It was like I was drowning,' he says. He had pulmonary oedema, an infliction that anybody who ventures to extreme altitude knows to be a risk.

Nimsdai had no choice but to descend to a lower altitude if he was to make a recovery, but whilst most people with pulmonary oedema would think twice about climbing high again, certainly in the same season, Nimsdai rested at a lower altitude just long enough to feel better again, and then returned to Everest and remarkably climbed to the summit, still with enough energy in reserve to rescue a climber on the descent. He stumbled across a lone climber, semi-conscious and barely able to speak, high in the Death Zone, and somehow, he managed to cajole, persuade and physically drag her down the mountain on a tight rope until she had strength enough to stand. Together they made it down to the safety of the high camp on the South Col, where exhausted, Nimsdai collapsed. Four days later he was back 'kicking doors' in Afghanistan and nobody, except Suchi, knew anything about his climb.

The following year, he was back on Everest again – this time on a Gurkha expedition. He climbed it once, blazing a trail and fixing the ropes with the Sherpas, and then a second time – this time sweeping down from the Everest's summit to the South Col and up the other side to the summit of Lhotse (the fourth highest mountain in the world and a part of the same massif) in a record time of 10 hours and 15 minutes. Not satisfied with this, he then took a couple of days' break to party hard, drinking and dancing with friends in the local mountain town of Namche Bazar, before heading to the fifth highest mountain in the world, Makalu. This he climbed with a small team from base camp to summit in a single push, leading from the front and trail-blazing through heavy snow and high winds. So, he climbed three of the world's eight-thousanders – Everest, Lhotse and Makalu – in five days. Another record.

Mindset and belief

This run of successes naturally served to develop Nimsdai's belief in his capability at extreme altitude. He recognized that there were technically better climbers who could outperform him at sea level, but above 8,000 metres he had the self-belief that he could climb to the summit of any mountain in the world – and fast. He had trailblazed through waist-deep snow, leaving experienced Sherpas in his wake. He had learned to make quick, high-risk decisions, and he understood the fine line between being courageous and foolhardy.

But this physical and mental prowess didn't come without commitment and hard work. Nimsdai talks about an ethos he had long applied in life: 'If I ever got up in the morning and told myself that I was going to do 300 push-ups that day, I made sure to do them, whole-heartedly, because to skip the effort would be to break a commitment, and breaking commitments led to failure.' His time in the military trained him to push beyond his psychological limits and shaped his thinking and belief toward the imperative to get the job done; any negativity was ignored. Or, if it couldn't be ignored, then he'd find a way to look at it through a different lens to turn it into a positive. In his words, he, 'attacked everything with positive thought'.

So now he asked himself, 'If I could take three of the world's largest mountains in five days, maybe I had it in me to climb the five tallest peaks in an equally impressive time: Everest, K2, Kanchenjunga, Lhotse and Makalu in, say, 80 days?' The idea gnawed at him for weeks until he decided to act upon it. He believed it possible – unfortunately, however, those around him weren't so sure. Eighty days was a long time to be on leave, his superiors told him. And anyway, it was too risky.

'Well, that's it then,' he thought, 'I'm going to quit.'

To be a soldier carries risks all of its own, but the military offered Nimsdai psychological security – structure, focus and loyalty. And then there was the small matter of a pension that he would no longer be entitled to; he was just a few years short of securing a guaranteed pension for life.

Interestingly, I was faced with a similar decision when I wanted to climb Everest. I was working for a magazine at the time, and the financial director made it very clear: I had a choice between my job and the mountain. I didn't want to give up my job and was very seriously worried about how I would pay the mortgage, but when I sat down and wrote my letter of resignation, I felt an overwhelming flood of freedom, knowing it was the right decision for me. So, I understand Nimsdai when he says that he felt liberated – though in his case, his resignation and new-found independence also made him even bolder. Rather than climbing the five tallest mountains in eighty days, he decided that he would climb the fourteen tallest mountains – all the eight-thousanders – in seven months. And so, Project Possible was born.

Planning and finance

Mountaineering is a risky game, and for the majority of people the very thought of climbing repeatedly into the Death Zone would seem to be inviting disaster. There are some risks in the mountains over which we have a degree of control; others, such as avalanche, over which we have no control – and at the end of the day it's a numbers game. But for Nimsdai, this was the least of his concerns. Much more worrying was how he was going to raise the funds. He needed £750,000, maybe more.

From the minute that Nimsdai's one year's notice was accepted by the ministry of Defence, he set two plans in motion. The first was the operational logistics of climbing these 14 mountains scattered across three countries: Nepal, Pakistan and China. Operations was something for which he was well trained and well positioned to put in place. He figured out when to climb each mountain, based on weather reports of the past five climbing seasons, and split Project Possible into three phases. The first, in Nepal, was to climb Annapurna, Dhaulagiri, Kanchenjunga, Everest, Lhotse and Makalu, in April and May. The second was to climb the mountains in Pakistan: Nanga Parbat, Gasherbrum I and II, K2 and Broad Peak, in July. And finally, he would return to Nepal to climb Manaslu in the autumn, before heading to China to climb Cho Oyu and Shishapangma. He had a number of connections in the climbing community in Nepal and pulled together a team of Nepalese climbers that he knew would be up to the task.

The second plan – critical to implement the first – was to raise the money. This was to prove a much greater challenge. Nimsdai had no experience in fund-raising but still he threw himself into it with the 100 per cent philosophy that had served him so well in every other aspect of his life. He decided that on three of the mountains – one from each phase – he would guide clients, to help pay the way. This was small fry, though, in comparison to the money he needed to raise through sponsorship. The work was relentless. Between his military commitments, he was on a constant and exhausting conveyor belt of train journeys, meetings and phone calls – usually with disappointing results. As time went on, his efforts intensified. He knew that he needed to build a profile and understood the power and reach of social media for this purpose, but he wasn't technically savvy – at least at the start. Just to prepare a couple of Project Possible posts, adding the relevant links and hashtags, sometimes took him a couple of hours, and he'd be up early at 4.00am most mornings to work on this before racing for a 7.00am train to London from his home on the south coast. He'd attend four or five meetings in a day, bolstering himself against false promises and rejections, and on the rare occasions he'd finish work before midnight, he'd open up his computer and write a series of follow-up emails before rounding off the day posting content on Instagram or Facebook.

By the turn of 2019, time running short if he was to climb that same year, he had accrued nowhere near the money that he needed. His wife, Suchi, never applied any emotional pressure, but none of us operates in a vacuum and the responsibility he felt for his parents, too, as the youngest son (traditionally the one to care for parents in Nepal) weighed heavy. He was under tremendous pressure, but not once did he think of quitting. Arguably, there might have been a halfway house: delaying until the following year – but he felt strongly that 2019 was the year to climb, while he was still physically and psychologically strong from his recent engagement in combat. And he knew that he couldn't afford to transfer any negativity to potential sponsors, even subconsciously; to instil faith in others, he must maintain faith in himself.

A small sum was donated by a businessman, another by a friend, and Nimsdai earned a helpful fee speaking at a corporate event. The UK's Nepalese community and a group of retired Gurkhas organized a Project Possible fund-raising drive and pensioners and veterans donated sums of £5, £10 and £20. But in the end, Nimsdai re-mortgaged his house. Nobody put their hands in their pockets at the fund-raising event at the Royal Geographical Society in London, at least not immediately. And as the countdown to Nimsdai's first climb approached, he had amassed around £115,000, barely enough to cover phase one. Relying on self-belief and momentum, he readied himself for the most ambitious operation of his life.

The team

'I trained on Annapurna,' says Nimsdai, 'no time before that.' At 8,091 metres, Annapurna is the tenth highest mountain in the world – and the deadliest. Its jumble of glaciers, seracs, crevasses and shark fin ridges, and its inherent instability combined with a temperamental climate and ferocious winds, mean that many climbers have fallen victim on its slopes. The ratio of successful ascents to fatalities on the mountain is around 35 per cent, higher even than K2 and Nanga Parbat. It was nonetheless the first of the 8,000-metre peaks to be climbed, in 1950, by a French expedition led by Maurice Herzog, and the first of Nimsdai's fourteen eight-thousanders.

Nimsdai had gathered his team, many of them friends or associates, all of them seasoned guides with a number of 8,000-metre peaks to their names – but the mountains ahead would offer very different challenges and he needed to know who would be best suited for what. Some mountains would require a team of climbers to break trail and fix lines on the steeper slopes from base camp to summit, while others he had climbed already; they were familiar, and likely would have ropes already fixed. On these mountains he would climb with just one companion. Annapurna, as one of the most challenging of the fourteen eight-thousanders, provided the perfect test scenario to assess players under pressure. He needed climbers with strength, climbers he could trust to keep their heads in dangerous situations, and climbers with an optimistic mindset. This last point was important for Nimsdai. He wanted people to be climbing for the love of it, not just for the money (although they would be paid well) – and people who felt pride in the Nepalese guiding community. This last point was one of his driving motivations. For Nimsdai, Project Possible was a way of championing the Nepali Sherpas who for too long had been the unsung heroes of the Himalayas, putting in the bulk of the back-breaking and often dangerous work to support expeditions at extreme altitude, while rarely receiving the credit they deserved. But for him to highlight their skills, he needed a team to share his philosophy: although comfortable in his role as leader and decision-maker, he didn't want dedicated followers, rather he wanted each individual to think for himself. In the Special Forces, each team was made up of expert warriors. Similarly, Nimsdai wanted each member of his team to operate as an expert climber with the capability of looking after himself in dangerous situations. He wanted them to be regarded as the Special Forces of high-altitude mountaineering. On Annapurna, Purja selected those who would be in his core team; those who would be on hand to provide back-up if required, and one Sherpa, Dawa, who would double check every detail of his expedition plans as they progressed.

Fourteen eight-thousanders

Annapurna lived up to its reputation. They had established Camp 2, the air was calm, the sun setting, and the team was relaxed, dancing and joking while the smell of fried chicken and rice wafted over the camp…when there was a deafening crack from somewhere above their heads, and an eruption of snow billowed down the mountain towards them. The men dived for cover in their tents. The snow smashed over them at full force, hammering and tearing at the canvas...and there was silence. They were spared.

The route they were climbing on Annapurna, however, now looked and felt too high risk. Thinking on his feet, Nimsdai utilized a drone he'd brought along for filming aerial shots as a reconnaissance tool, hovering it over a series of icy ridges and examining the captured footage on his mobile phone. The alternative route that he chose was far more technical, but less prone to avalanche: the Dutch Rib, a narrow ridge of powder snow and ice, precipitous slopes either side. Nimsdai and his team fixed the rope and trailblazed most of the route, taking it in turns to lead all the way to the summit. It was 23 April 2019, and the clock was ticking.

The next mountain in line was Dhaulagiri, one that Nimsdai had already climbed. Three members of the team had gone on ahead to fix ropes and establish camps on the mountain, but what they didn't know is that they would have to wait for Nimsdai and the rest of the team longer than expected. Annapurna climbed, there was a call for a rescue; a climber was stranded high on the mountain. Nimsdai and his team volunteered to help, and attaching themselves one by one on long lines to the underbelly of a helicopter, they were swooped up into the biting Himalayan sky.

The delay meant that they missed a favourable weather window on Dhaulagiri – and then bad weather blew in. Their ropes were buried in newly fallen snow, their tents beaten flat in the wind – and the mood of those at base camp was low. But from this difficult situation came some good. Any team needs a collective sense of purpose if it's to perform at its best, but the players within the team also need rest and relaxation. Now was the time. They withdrew from the mountain for a whole week to regroup, to party hard, as is Nimsdai's style, to drink and dance, and returned recharged for the challenge ahead. The other good thing that emerged from the bad was that the story of the rescue on Annapurna was posted on social media. People woke up to the team's capabilities and Nimsdai's following grew.

Stunningly, Nimsdai climbed Annapurna, Dhaulagiri, Kanchenjunga, Everest, Lhotse and Makalu in just 31 days. Then in just 23 days, he climbed all the eight-thousanders in Pakistan: K2, Nanga Parbat, Broad Peak, G1 and G2. The first two phases of Project Possible completed, he then returned to England in August, for the duration of the monsoon.

Nimsdai might have lacked certain skills in social media at the start of his project, but he made it a priority to learn and his newly-acquired communication skills paid off. While still in the Himalayan village of Lukla, famous for its tiny runway perched on the edge of a cliff, he had successfully negotiated a sponsorship deal on his smart phone. But the need to raise money didn't stop. As soon as his plane touched down at Heathrow, he was on the sponsorship conveyor belt once again. He didn't go home for a week.

I was fascinated by Nimsdai's story. I was commissioned to write an article and jumped in the car and spent an afternoon with him in the house he re-mortgaged to kick off the first phase of his project. He greeted me bare foot in comfy trackies and a T-shirt, and with three of his media team we sat in the kitchen and ate a traditional Nepalese plate of momos – something that took me straight back to our cook tent at Camp 2 on Everest.

At this point in time, Nimsdai was two-thirds of the way to heartily proving me wrong, and I was delighted. He admitted that he had felt a little fear at the thought of climbing the Savage Mountain, K2. 'But in the event it wasn't as difficult as the other mountains,' he says, 'because we climbed it "normally", stopping at Camps 2 and 4 to rest.' Astonishingly, he climbed Makalu, Kanchenjunga, GI and Broad Peak, in a single push from base camp to summit.

This can be regarded as a paradigm shift in mountaineering, taking the ultra-marathon to the extremist of altitudes. The late Doug Scott, pioneer mountaineer and first Briton to climb Everest, by way of a new route, the South West Face, in 1975, said of Nimsdai, 'He is a phenomenon, a natural acclimatizer, a marathon man at altitude.'

Nonetheless, Nimsdai didn't escape criticism. It is the tradition of the pioneering breed to always seek the harder challenge, which in mountaineering has meant forging new routes, foregoing siege-style tactics for lightweight Alpine ascents, and eschewing bottled oxygen. No matter that the harder challenge might be climbing 14 eight-thousanders in seven months, even if by way of established routes, with Sherpa support and oxygen, and where practicable, the employment of helicopters to travel from one mountain to another. On the point of oxygen, the choice to use it was very deliberate on Nimsdai's behalf. He knew that he wouldn't have had the strength to rescue the woman stranded at high altitude on his first ascent of Everest had he not been breathing supplementary oxygen, and didn't want to be compromised in this regard in the future. The Project Possible team was involved in four rescues in the course of climbing the 14 eight-thousanders.

In late August 2019, Nimsdai flew to Kathmandu to climb the remaining three eight-thousanders: Cho Oyu, Manaslu and

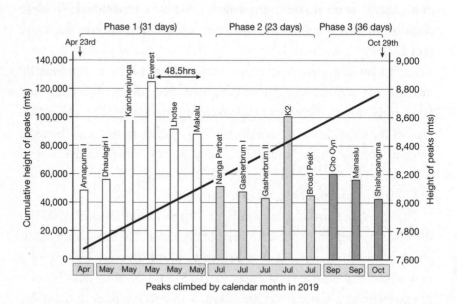

Peaks climbed by calendar month in 2019

Shishapangma – relative molehills by comparison to those already climbed. There was heart-stopping suspense when we heard his mother had been rushed to hospital and was in intensive care. Communication stopped. The mission stopped. Until with relief he posted to the world, 'Guess what, my mum's operation was successful this afternoon, she's OK now so I'm OK.'

On 7th September, he returned to the mountains, to Manaslu. His unshakable belief in his ability to complete Project Possible had got him thus far. Now, others believed in him, too. Another sponsor stepped on board to help him over the finish line. 'This project is about pushing myself to what is possible within human endurance, but I will not fight Mother Nature. I respect her and in doing so I will be able to continue to completion of Project Possible,' says Nimsdai. He climbed Manaslu and Cho Oyu, and then following more suspense when there was a question over whether or not the Chinese government would grant him a permit to climb his fourteenth and final mountain, Shishapangma, he was finally given the stamp of approval and climbed that, too. The date, 29 October 2019. He beat his own seven-month target and climbed all fourteen eight thousand metre peaks in just six months and six days, shaving more than seven years off the existing record.

K2 winter ascent

Inevitably COVID-19 scuppered many of Nimsdai's plans for 2020, but he wasn't idle. He wrote and published his book, *Beyond Possible*, about the climbing of the 14 eight-thousanders, and quickly focused on his next challenge – to climb the Savage Mountain, K2, in the winter. K2 was the only eight-thousand metre peak that hadn't been climbed in the winter months, and not for the lack of effort on behalf of the world's hardiest mountaineers. In December 1987, a predominantly Polish expedition, comprising a few Canadians and Britons too, made the first attempt to climb K2 in the winter. At the time, Poles dominated high-altitude mountaineering, and an exceptionally experienced group of alpinists known as the Ice Warriors specialized in winter climbing. They made an astonishing seven first winter ascents of 8,000-metre peaks in a span of eight years, but they failed on K2. Mountaineer Roger Mear, who has walked to the South Pole and made the first winter ascent of the long and difficult Cassin Ridge on Mount Denali in Alaska, was on the team, and says, 'I'd never go back again – it's far too dangerous.' There were several more expeditions that made winter attempts through the years, but not even one of them managed to reach Camp 4 on the shoulder of K2 – the critical high camp from which to launch a summit bid.

In short, K2 in the winter is brutal, considered by far the most challenging eight-thousander because of the technical climbing required to reach the top. 'Some of the slopes are almost 70 degrees,' says Nimsdai, 'and you are climbing on blue ice or on rock.' And in the winter, the temperatures can fall as low as minus 65 degrees Celsius.

By late December 2020, Nimsdai and his team had successfully established Camp 2, and together with Mingma G Sherpa, who was leading another team on the mountain, fixed ropes almost to Camp 3, before returning to base camp for a short rest. The time that Nimsdai and Mingma G had shared together gave them an opportunity to chat. They were climbing at similar speeds, both with the objective of climbing K2 in the winter, and, and in an unusual move in the climbing world, they decided to collaborate. 'Gone are the days when it's for only one individual,' says Nimsdai, 'everybody is working hard over there, let's share everything. Let's unite and conquer this, and let's send a really positive message to the rest of the world.'

There was one incident that would have had most climbers scuttling home fast: Nimsdai climbed back up to Camp 2 to discover a wreckage site. A storm had ripped through the tents and all their equipment left in preparation for the summit push – sleeping bags, mattresses, heated shoe insoles, summit gloves, summit base layers, paragliding equipment (yes, Nimsdai planned to jump off the top) and cooking equipment – had been blown off the mountain. 'It just made our plan a bit tougher,' says Nimsdai.

In a remarkable collaborative effort, Nimsdai's team, together with Mingma G Sherpa's team, combined forces to fix ropes on the upper reaches of the mountain and, on 16 January 2021, waited just below the summit to form a group, before slowly stepping onto the top together, singing the Nepali national anthem. One Sherpa from a commercial expedition, Sona Sherpa, also joined the effort. There were ten climbers in total: Mingma G Sherpa, Nimsdai, Sona Sherpa, Mingma David Sherpa, Mingma Tenzi Sherpa, Geljen Sherpa, Pemchiri Sherpa, Dawa Temba Sherpa, Dawa Tenjin Sherpa and Kili Pemba Sherpa. 'This Nepalese winter K2 expedition is for the nation,' Mingma G wrote on social media.

This long sought-after achievement adds a stunning new chapter to mountaineering history and highlights the strength, skills and collaborative and organizational capabilities of Nepalese climbers, who for so long have been the backbone of Himalayan expeditions but with very little recognition. Conscious of the magnitude of this historic moment – one shared with every member of the team – Nimsdai held back a couple of days before announcing that he had climbed without supplementary oxygen. On Project Possible, he chose to use supplementary oxygen, but K2 was different. It was a tough decision to make, for three reasons. First, he hadn't acclimatized as he would have liked – he had only slept at Camp 2 when normally a climber would sleep at or at least touch Camp 4 before making a summit push without oxygen. Secondly, he had three frost-nipped fingers from fixing ropes high on the mountain – and oxygen keeps fingers and toes warm. And thirdly, he says, 'I was leading an expedition of this incredible superhuman team, and once they took oxygen, they are going to be even [more] super human and I was thinking, can I still lead this group from the front?' If one of the team had to wait for him, it could cost them their fingers and toes, or more. Weighed up against this, though,

Nimsdai had the experience to know exactly how his body responded to altitude. He took a calculated risk, and it paid off: 'JOB DONE!' he posted on Instagram. K2 had been climbed in the winter with no supplementary oxygen.

So, what is his secret? 'You've got to love what you're doing,' he says. 'As a kid, my only dream was to be a Gurkha. Once I got into the Gurkhas, I found out about the Special Forces. I didn't join the Special Forces for any money or name or fame, it was just a pure love with a passion. And from there, giving up my prestigious career – I must say that – and my pension, and completely entering this mountaineering field, there was a love for me for the mountains. Of course, talent is one thing but if you want to be number one in the world you've got to be working harder than eight billion population. A lot of people see the success, but behind this success there is blood, sweat and tears. Success is not a coincidence – you've got to be self-disciplined and self-motivated. More than that, your purpose should be bigger than you. When you have all these things, you can always achieve the impossible.'

References

1. Sherpa – a member of a Himalayan people living on the borders of Nepal and Tibet, renowned for their skill in mountaineering
2. The Bhutia are a community of Sikkimese people of Tibetan ancestry
3. Crampons – traction devices attached to footwear to improve mobility on snow and ice

For more information see *Beyond Possible: One Soldier, Fourteen Peaks – My life in the Death Zone* by Nimsdai Purja, Hodder & Stoughton, 2020

CHAPTER EIGHT

A Strategy Executed – Saving a Pottery and Building a Brand

Every pot that is crafted required hands to be spoiled.

Anonymous

Perhaps unsurprisingly for a designer best known for her homely polka dot mugs, Emma Bridgewater's family and business life have run hand in hand from the start, intertwined with one another in a wonderfully creative, colourful mesh. Magical in so many ways, and yet just occasionally tipping into the chaotic. But that's family life. Refreshingly, Emma Bridgewater is quick to chat about the subject that in a work context is so often the elephant in the room: children. Both the importance of their upbringing, and the inner conflict so often felt when time is spent away from those you love in order to make a living. 'We acknowledge life is spread too thinly,' she says. 'Obviously work is more than just work if it's remotely rewarding, but there's quite a lot of other stuff to get done.' Once a party to 'the boring, macho, 80s thing of seeing how many hours you can put in', she says, 'everything changes when you've got a kid. I just wanted to get the job done, because I wanted to get home for the kids' bedtime.'

Emma Bridgewater has four children and is one of eight siblings herself. One of her sisters is disabled and her mother had the most terrible riding accident that left her with severe brain injuries and in institutional care for 22 years. 'There's all that family stuff that falls heavy or light by chance,' she says. 'I had a lot of it very early on and it was exhausting beyond your worst nightmares.' Yet not only has she survived, she's the owner of a thriving global brand bearing her name, and even now in her 50s is still ambitious for growth.

As an English Literature graduate, it might have been a natural choice for Bridgewater to pursue a career as a literary agent – something she holds a mild hankering for to this day. A life among books would have suited her, she says, but the pull of entrepreneurship was stronger. Her father had his own business; he was a publisher of educational career books, something 'my brain sort of skids away from', says Bridgewater. But as a sixth former and undergraduate she worked stints in his office and observed a sense of order that led to the successful sale of his business on the public markets when she was at university – she saw first-hand the impact structure and organization had on a company's trajectory. She then worked for two knitwear designers who were 'disorderly but creative, their business much more fun', and thought that it must be possible, somehow, to mesh the best of these two businesses into one.

How the business started

Bridgewater was consciously looking for something that she could really put her heart into, to build a business she considered worthwhile, when she happened upon an idea while looking for a birthday present for her mother. The story illustrates how the threads that weave through her family and business life were intertwined from the very beginning. She wanted to give her mother something personal, something to show her mother that she wanted to be with her, despite it being a time when they were mostly apart. She fell upon the idea of a pair of cups and saucers, conjuring up the image of their sitting together, chatting and drinking coffee in the family kitchen – and it wasn't easy to find what she was looking for. The cups and saucers were all too angular and heavy for her liking, too dull, or worst of all, too formal. None of the china bore any relation to the cosy shapes and colourful mishmash picked up from market stalls, Granny's cupboards and family holidays, then displayed in a messy, relaxed sort of way on the shelves of her mother's comfortably chipped painted dresser.

Bridgewater asked herself, where was the easy-going everyday china – colourful, relaxed and fun to use? And in that question was the germ of her business. 'Suddenly I could see it,' she says. 'I knew what it looked like, and I knew that I wanted to make it. The vision in the china shop of the future was vivid. There would be a kitchen dresser, laden with mugs and plates and bowls of mismatched patterns that echoed the sense of my mother's dresser.'

The vision is all-important, she argues. Today when people approach Bridgewater for advice, her first question is always, 'is there a vision of your business? Project yourself forward. What will your life be like? Walk me around it. What is it? So, it's studio. Describe me that studio. Where is it?' From experience she understands this to be the first and most important step. 'If you've got a clear idea of what it is you want to create,' she says, 'you can amass the skills. All you actually need is the determination to achieve that, and the focus. Success is in finding the vision sufficiently compelling and then gripping on and never letting go.'

Bridgewater had no formal education in business or marketing, but her strength was to observe and extrapolate the best from others she worked for and alongside, and to listen. 'People are great. If you ask a sensible question of the right person, they will take enormous pain to help you find the answer,' she says; something she's happy to do for others today.

When Bridgewater had her germ of an idea, that was it – an idea, nothing else. She hadn't the first clue about manufacturing. 'I was talking to a friend,' she says. 'He was a graphic designer, and I said I've got this idea, pottery, I want it refined and nice like Wedgwood primeware from the 1820s, and he said "stop right there, it's called Stoke-on-Trent. There are still some potteries there; I was up there only last week." And he literally gave me one man's name and number.' There was advice not so welcomed as well. 'Early on someone sat me down and said, "you know that business isn't awfully nice", and I was thinking, I'm already not liking this conversation. "And," he said, "it will get complicated. Once there's money involved, people show their true colours – friendships will be sacrificed, you'll have some terrible times – are you actually up for this?"'

Making the first products

But these were early days and Bridgewater was not about to be put off. The man recommended by her friend, whose number Bridgewater had taken care to write down on the back of a cigarette packet, was Sam: a talented craftsman and model maker, and the key to unlocking Bridgewater's business. She set about drawing a set of shapes that she hoped he would be able to make for her – a mug that was the centrepiece, cosy and commanding, a bowl that could be comfortably cupped in two hands, a jug and a serving dish. All based on a deep love of what she understood to be essentially English (and probably specifically Staffordshire) earthenware, although there was a touch of the Scottish and French that crept into her designs as well. She took these drawings with her to Stoke-on-Trent in the West Midlands, to 'The Potteries' as the city is commonly known, home to Royal Doulton, Wedgwood and Minton, and a million miles from the comfortable middle-class kitchens of Oxford and London that are so familiar to Emma Bridgewater.

'When I first arrived in Stoke, what moved me was the dereliction and all the empty potteries, hundreds of them of all shapes and sizes,' says Bridgewater. 'The industry was imploding, but in Sam's business I found the tail end of an amazing tradition, knowledge and enthusiasm.'

Sam was able to take Bridgewater's somewhat naïve collection of drawings and translate them into real three-dimensional objects of simple beauty and practicality. He brought her drawings to life, and in so doing reciprocated Bridgewater's offer of a business relationship that was to define the strategy of Emma Bridgewater the business – and revive a failing pottery in the process. 'I didn't understand the mechanics and economics of the business at this point,' says Bridgewater, 'but it was very obvious that nobody in the factory understood its audience anymore.' They were making teapots with no lids, saucers with no cups, dinner services that might have made a desirable wedding gift in the 1950s. 'I came from Oxford, understanding what north Oxford kitchens were like,' says Bridgewater, 'thinking how weird that they're not making any of the kit we need.' The genius of Emma Bridgewater was to marry the manufacturing skills of Stoke-on-Trent potteries with the contemporary and evolving tastes of the commercial retail markets, initially in the wealthy southern counties of England.

It started small. Bridgewater scraped together £450 making canapés for drinks parties and happily handed the money to Sam, in return for a sample batch, potted and biscuit fired, that she collected and drove down to Brixton, where she was living at the time with a photographer boyfriend. Between jobs he leant a hand, experimenting with glazing and firing the pieces in a kiln in the bathroom, placing the successful ones to one side to be photographed and selling the remainder in Covent Garden's Jubilee Market on a Sunday. 'A horrible, hungry, wet, cold winter it was too,' says Bridgewater.

She twisted the arm of many a friend and relative to buy these early products while she focused on putting together a leaflet with photographs and a price list, sending it to some 120 shops across the south of England, in Bath, Bristol, Oxford, Canterbury and London. Cash flow was an issue at the start, but she managed to persuade her early customers to agree terms of 28 days while she negotiated a 30-day payment arrangement with Sam. Still, it was expensive and exhausting driving a hired delivery van the length and breadth of the motorway network across southern England. She says, 'I remember really wishing I hadn't recruited a shop in Hereford West.'

There is little doubt that Emma Bridgewater's business wouldn't have taken off in the way that it did had the shape of the mug in particular not been so universally appealing to those aspiring to a relaxed, informal way of living. But a further differentiator was the patterns with which they were decorated. Bridgewater unearthed, researched and brought back to life a tradition that had long since died – sponge printing, with its repeat pattern akin to potato prints on fabric, that had been used by Scottish potteries and then the Staffordshire potteries in the early- to mid-nineteenth century. Not only did it produce patterns that were both attractive and oddly contemporary – her famous polka dots, cut flowers, stars or a single hare – but it provided a subliminal connection to people of old, a link to tradition that customers warmed to. Bridgewater experimented with the technique with no knowledge of how it was done 200 years ago, first using the hard root of natural sponges, difficult to source, and finally settling upon furnishing foam, cutting it into shapes using a soldering iron, 'clouds of toxic fumes filling the room'.

This early DIY period was essential for developing designs and patterns and truly understanding the making of the product, but it was also a transitional period in Bridgewater's mind; she quickly learned that she had no interest in doing any part of the making process, and taught and outsourced the sponge printing to three women in Sam's factory. Meanwhile she had moved to a cousin's run-down but conveniently positioned house in Chelsea until 'eventually', she says, 'a float from Stoke-on-Trent barged its way around the square and unloaded into the wrong basement, and I got shopped to the council who came to close me down. I flung myself on the mercy of this nice guy who turned up to find out what on earth was going on,' she says, 'and he helped me find an industrial unit – an ex-paper-bag factory – off the Fulham Road.'

If it all sounds a bit haphazard, it was. The vision was bright and vividly coloured but the learning curve steep. About six months after writing her first invoice, the bank manager called her in and demanded to know what was going on. She had effectively been trading out of her own current account. A friendly accountant was appalled by the liability she was creating and strenuously advised her to cease trading immediately, but Bridgewater wasn't about to do that: she wanted a business overdraft. Naturally, the bank wanted a business plan, and with no clue how to present one she once again reached out to someone who might be able to help her and asked a friend, Marcus Pollen, to put something on paper. Marcus managed to extract some sense of order from the chaos and capture Bridgewater's optimism: he stressed the ordering and indeed re-ordering from some 120 shops, but most importantly he captured Bridgewater's confidence in her product – she was successfully selling her earthenware at roughly twice the price of other comparable products on the market, and got the overdraft she wanted.

Growing bigger

Marriage came soon after to a man she met at a trade show. A designer himself, Matthew Rice ran an illustrative stationary business alongside Bridgewater for a while, though for Emma there was only ever one game in town and that was the pottery. Shortly after they were married, Emma and Matthew formed a partnership with Emma's friend Marcus Pollen, who was to be the business brain. It wasn't long before Emma's vision of a kitchen dresser laden with mugs, jugs and bowls of mismatched patterns was realized in two shops, one on Fulham Road and one on Marylebone High Street, while she still sold through some 120 shops including Liberty, General Trading Company and John Lewis.

They ran the partnership for about 10 years. Emma and Matthew moved to Norfolk to be nearer her mother. The two of them worked on designs, the aim being that with every new collection the customer 'entirely recognizes and feels comfortable with it and at the same time is entirely charmed by the new relevant thing', says Bridgewater. 'We work really hard at that.' They created and manned a lot of trade fair stands, in France and the US as well as in England, styling and designing the catalogues throughout – but neither of them actually ran the company at this time. 'Given that it was when I was having babies and mum had her accident, poor Marcus didn't really get very much of my focus – but he kept things going,' says Bridgewater.

There were two major events that propelled Emma Bridgewater to a different level. The first was that Sam's business ran into trouble and she and Matthew decided to borrow against their house in order to step in and buy the big Victorian pottery. The general consensus among friends was that this was high risk and a mistake; that it would be more prudent to stick to what they knew as designers and marketers. 'They were right,' says Emma, 'and they were wrong. We never saw the nimble design and marketing studio in Central London we might have been.' Bridgewater suspects that had they taken this route the company might have grown quicker, but on the other hand she feels that her personal fulfilment came from investing in the manufacturing side of the business as well. 'It's been the greatest privilege of my life,' she says, 'to have been able to create jobs and invest in the traditions and values embodied in Stoke-on-Trent.'

Ironically, as many competitors were trading in for cheap equivalents manufactured in less binding jurisdictions, Bridgewater invested more deeply in home-produced products. 'The thing they were throwing aside has been at the very heart of my business: the expertise of Staffordshire potting, its tradition and the people who hold it, keeping afloat something that was definitely sinking – that's the thing that's motivated me for 35 years. Businesses shouldn't exist primarily and first and last to furnish their shareholders with ever more profit,' she adds. 'Shareholders should be a little tiny bit more mindful about what the company represents and does.'

The second event was a realization that the company didn't have a strategy, it wasn't growing – and they had four children and a house badly in need of a new roof. 'When Michael arrived,' she says, referring to their youngest child, 'something changed in me and I could feel a rising determination to make the company much larger, more profitable, and more powerful. But for some time I wavered, totally unsure how to go about taking this momentous step.'

It is reassuring that a woman clearly so successful, appointed a CBE for her services to industry, should, like so many mothers, have a little wobble at the thought of returning to work full time after taking a break to look after her children. Indeed it's equally reassuring that her inspiration should come from another extraordinary woman who threw passion and hard work into a creation of a different sort: a garden famous for its snowdrops, near Holt in Norfolk. Her name was Billa Harrod. Bridgewater went to one of Billa's 'snowdrop mornings' one wintry February day and in the hallway of her house stood a round table, in the middle of which was a huge, purple lustre punch bowl stuffed full with snowdrops. 'I asked her how they all sat so prettily – why didn't the middle ones drown?' says Bridgewater, 'and she showed me that they stood on sodden, bunched-up newspaper. It was a piece of perfection. I thought about her determination to make good things happen in life, and the fog I had been in cleared. If I wanted to make the company work, if I wanted to make good things happen, it was time to set aside my placatory habits. I would have to be uncompromising, like Billa. That's all.'

As it happened, Marcus Pollen was ready to move on to set up a business of his own, so Bridgewater bought back the shares she had parted with in the early years, and threw her heart and soul into energizing the brand, while Matthew stayed closer to home and his parents moved nearby to help with the children. It was exhausting and at times heart-breaking, tearing herself away from 'the sweet peas and the roses' and driving the huge triangle between their home in rural North Norfolk, the potteries in the West Midlands and London, where for a long while the commercial office was in a 'dark and smelly basement below the Fulham Road shop'. She was driving 50,000 miles in a year, but it was an imperative part of the business strategy.

The observation Bridgewater made right at the start – that the potteries had lost contact with the market – might still apply if there wasn't a constant line of communication between the commercial and retail and the manufacturers. 'You've got to be in the market,' says Bridgewater. 'It's always been the principle that the commercial office in London understands what the customer wants, and the factory makes it. Each is to be aligned with the other, led always by the commercial demand.' Their commercial office could have been in another vibrant city but the business was started in the capital, and in reality it was probably the best location to recruit people with the required commercial skills. 'We want crash hot merchandisers,' says Bridgewater, 'people who have been trained and disciplined within the best retailers to come and do a stint in a creative company and bring some value. You pay what it takes.'

The other issue that Bridgewater tackled head on was inventory control, about which 'the factory had grown very sleepy', she says. 'We imported absolute state-of-the-art product development control, so that we've got precisely the right things on the shelf at precisely the right hour of the right day.'

Over the course of three or four years, Bridgewater made considerable headway. She brought on board an effective commercial director and a financial controller, and eventually gained some real insight into what was happening in the factory, where, she says, 'there was a mixture of fantastic loyalty and predictable dishonesty'. To assert better control throughout the company, half the staff from the factory office were moved down to the commercial office in London, now on Fulham High Street. One wonders if those early words of advice from a friend were resonating in her ears: 'you know that business isn't awfully nice'. Sales tripled, but there were difficult partings, and the factory could still be hard to govern.

At one point, the Potters' Union requested an interview. 'We were paying over their recommendations and had no safety issues,' says Bridgewater, 'but the tone, the atmosphere, of the meeting shocked and haunted me. It made me realize what I had blithely ignored up to that point: that to some people, my project – my business – was offensive.

No matter that I employed 70 people at the time. Their attitude was not, as I assumed it must be, *that's great, how can we help you make that 140 jobs?* Instead they simply hated me for being a boss and sought to gain what controls they might within the company.'

Bridgewater doesn't lack self-reflection. She could see why she made them feel hot and furious. 'I hated my privileged situation at that moment and felt apologetic and confused. But my embarrassment passed, and when it had, I still wanted to make jobs and try and save a small part of this beleaguered industry. It seems that there is still a need – and also exciting scope – to develop a dynamic relationship between the unions who bring their proud history, traditions and skills, and entrepreneurs keen to make new products in this country.' She freely admits that teamwork is one of the most joyful and yet also one of the hardest things to get right. 'The difficulty of being on two sites – HQ in London and factory and warehouse in Stoke – is that bad management can fall apart all the time – blame, blame, blame. It's difficult to get everyone moving in the same direction,' she says, 'and yet we do.'

Taking a step back

Eventually, though, the long car journeys, the long hours and the worry of running the business began to take their strain. 'Stress is one of those things you don't believe in until it sneaks up on you,' she says. Worryingly, she suffered physical pain that was gradually immobilizing her. It was diagnosed as rheumatoid arthritis and she started treatment (which has many of the same side effects as chemotherapy), still driving hundreds of miles every week until the hideousness of the nausea forced her to stop.

One weekend she absolutely understood that she had to change her pattern of work if she was to recover. She and Matthew had been discussing how to move forward, and by the Sunday evening they had informed every employee that Matthew would be taking charge of the company. Bridgewater says, 'The children looked at me and said, "Why have you taken so long?"' She was able to undergo her treatment and within a couple of years she was in remission. The family was also in a position to move to Oxfordshire, markedly shortening the commute to Stoke-on-Trent and London.

As it turned out, Matthew proved that he was more than capable of stepping into Emma's shoes. He was at the helm for about eight years and was able to dramatically improve the team. Then, in 2015, they took on a managing director, Julia Cove-Smith, to run the business while the two of them remained in charge of design. As Design Director, Emma now works part-time and looks incredibly fit and well, able to create time to exercise and rest. 'You could say that we are two entrepreneurs who should have stepped away a bit sooner than we did,' says Bridgewater, 'mainly because we didn't have the money and didn't want to raise the capital or sell shares'.

But the business employs more than 400 'excellent people', says Bridgewater, mostly in Stoke-on-Trent, where she opened a vibrant factory outlet which, in a year not hit by a pandemic, draws tourists to the city and welcomes some 50,000 people a year through the door. There is a factory tour, a café, a studio where people can decorate their own pottery and, perhaps not surprisingly, a book festival in June. Running parallel with this enriching retail experience where buyers can see the products being made and understand exactly their provenance, Emma Bridgewater also sells directly to the customer online. It's a winning combination and one that has turned out to be extremely resilient too. The company was one of the earlier adopters of the internet, and as such it was well-primed for the unexpected in March 2020. Just before the Covid outbreak, Emma Bridgewater's sales were split roughly half and half between internet sales and retail outlets. When shops closed overnight, so half its business closed with them. Covid also put paid to Emma Bridgewater's two shops in London, on the Fulham Road and Marylebone High Street. To add salt to the wound, disruptions in supply chains meant there was no delivery of clay and the factory was forced to close for several weeks. Bridgewater and her senior team immediately took a pay cut. Fortunately, though, the company warehouses were full to the brim of spring and summer goods, and when clay was once again delivered, they were able to get the factory back up and running to manufacture goods for the autumn and winter. 'And wonderfully,' says Bridgewater, 'our customers migrated to the internet and bought directly from our website.'

As has been a theme throughout this book, the Emma Bridgewater brand is what it is because of extraordinarily hard work and, as Bridgewater would say, 'sticking with it'. 'It's been gruelling,' she says. 'If you want to make things happen, there's no two ways about it – you are going to have to work very hard.' Reflecting on her years with Matthew, she says 'there hasn't been quite enough demarcation between life and business'. Sadly, these two extraordinary creatives have recently divorced. 'We racked up 30 years of having lots of fun and I firmly believe we'll be good friends again. But it's horrible, and incredibly sad, and I do think that working together is very abrasive to a relationship. In the end you're too much the whip-cracker over each other and that's really unsuitable.'

But through it all, Bridgewater has shown the true resilience of an entrepreneur whose business isn't going to fade away. 2020 was a year of massive change for Emma Bridgewater, and not just as a result of the pandemic. The business had always been family-owned, but when Emma and Matthew went their separate ways, an investor bought Matthew's shares and Emma invested hard, while still holding an unusually high proportion of shares in the company. She expanded the factory and warehouse in Stoke-on-Trent, and built an in-house design studio alongside the commercial office in Fulham, employing four young designers (a role that had once been just hers and Matthew's). So, she now has a design and marketing studio in London, but importantly, she has her biggest passion, a factory in Stoke as well. 'It's all much more co-ordinated now,' says Bridgewater. This, even when the designers have been working from home for much of the year. 'And undoubtedly the development of our retail offering online and on social media has been crucial to our success.' A streamlined business and the immediacy of social media enables Bridgewater to be aligned with her customers not just from one season to the next but with the sunshine and falling rain of a particular week. Dandelions come into flower and Emma Bridgewater's homely mugs decorated with a pretty dandelion pattern pop up on Instagram.

'One way or another,' says Bridgewater, 'I will always ensure the brand is future proof. It's not to do with the money; it is to do with prosperity. It is to do with the people and the pride. It's about emotional and transactional connection with the customers.' She continues, 'My impulse when I started was to find the most loving gift I could think of for my mum. That sweet impulse that we all have, to demonstrate our love and give thoughtful presents, is right at the heart of the business.'

In the last decade or so, Emma Bridgewater has grown between 10 and 15 per cent every year, and remarkably, during the COVID-19 pandemic, it grew by 25 per cent. It might be an assumption that a creative company such as Emma Bridgewater finds a natural ceiling, 'but stand in a Waitrose car park and think about it', says Bridgewater. 'There are a lot of people there who don't yet know the name Emma Bridgewater. It's our job to find them, get through to them, and sell to them.'

CHAPTER NINE

Global Strategy Execution in a Multinational Corporation

A laser is a weak source of energy...but with a laser, you can drill a hole in a diamond or wipe out cancer. When you focus a company, you can create the same effect.

Al Ries, marketing expert and author

It is a rare achievement to take a large and established global company within a highly competitive market and more than double its growth within five years, but that is exactly what John Clarke, head of the Future Group and then President of GSK Consumer Healthcare, did between the years 2006 and 2011. At the start of his tenure, growth for Consumer Healthcare was at a sluggish 2 to 3 per cent; the business was ticking over with the launch of one or two new products a year, or none at all. It was questionable whether it would survive. Clarke and his team turned the company around to the point that it was launching 40 to 50 new products year on year; growth more than trebled to an average 10 per cent a year, growing 60 per cent in the 2006–2011 period from £3 billion to £5 billion in sales, resulting in GSK Consumer Healthcare becoming the leader in its field.

GlaxoSmithKline (GSK) is a large organization and Consumer Healthcare is a major business unit within it, with sales of £9bn in 2019. The unit sells well-known brands such as Aquafresh, Sensodyne, Voltaren and Panadol, as well as a number of other over-the-counter medicines.

It is a challenging business; it requires substantial R&D investment and faces stringent regulatory approval processes – which may vary in different countries. It also has increasingly demanding consumers and highly consolidated retail channels, and, if it is to be competitive, short cycle times for new product development. To add to the challenges it was, until the early 2000s, handicapped by a global structure that allowed a high degree of local market autonomy, which could very easily result in the fracturing of brand equity through poor timing, misaligned product launches, or ideas that simply hadn't been thoroughly thought through. The result: poor growth and a danger of stagnation.

GSK brought in John Clarke

There was acknowledgement that the company wasn't growing fast enough, and in an effort to rectify this, in 2004 a decision was made by the then president, Jack Ziegler, to completely change the way of working: essentially, to scrap the old model and start afresh with a blank sheet of paper. The decision was to drive innovation hard and to centralize marketing and R&D for its big global brands, such as Lucozade and Aquafresh, into a new, innovative global organization within Consumer Healthcare, appropriately called the Future Group. Says Dr Tom Robbins, then a Director of Innovation in the Future Group, now lecturer in innovation at Dublin City University, 'What GSK did then is what loads of companies are only just coming around to now.' The man brought in to head up the Future Group was the charismatic and experienced leader John Clarke, who was at the time general manager of GSK Consumer Healthcare Europe.

'Innovation was the name of the game,' explains Clarke. 'The strategy was to deliberately align innovation to new growth; our job to get innovative products to market, fast.' And this message he shouted loud and clear, most importantly to those who would be coming up with the ideas. 'He would come to a lot of meetings I was running around the world,' says Dr Robbins, 'and he'd say, *"If you're working on innovation, there is nothing more important for you to be working on than that."* I haven't seen that too often before or since.'

Importantly, though, while recognizing and encouraging talent in his team, John Clarke also recognized that GSK Consumer Healthcare wasn't so very different from its competitors. It had broadly similar asset holdings as its competitors, as well as similar resources, brands and operation capabilities. In the words of business writer Tom Peters – clearly an inspiration for Clarke – there was a lot of 'same-same'. Clarke understood that to be successful they needed to find a point of difference from other companies, and that difference, put in place in a very deliberate and systematic way, was the implementation of the strategy. Put simply, once having established the strategy, he ensured the company's single most important objective was to be better, faster and more efficient at *implementing* that strategy than its competitors. This *implementation of strategy* he regarded as a strategy in its own right.

To meet John Clarke for the first time, it's clear that he is a man of precision and discipline – qualities that define both his professional and personal life. Of an age when most of his school friends will have thickened slightly around the waist, he is youthfully slim. The morning that we met he had been to the gym first thing as, I was to learn, he did every morning. He is both a 'doer' and a measurer of actions. At the start of each year he schedules his gym entries for the 12 months ahead and checks his progress at regular intervals. He's also an accountant by training; he understands that work in the commercial world must translate into money and profit. And, as a New Zealander, he's fanatical about rugby. 'Probably where I developed much of my thinking,' he says. 'It's all about the combination of the totality rather than the individuals in the team. Collective effort. We wouldn't come off the pitch unless we'd given everything.'

Clarke challenged mediocrity and complacency every step of the way, and ensured that he had the very best possible team around him. Just as he regarded the implementation of strategy as a strategy in its own right, so too he regarded each component of the strategy –

advertising development, new product development and R&D – as a strategy in its own right, and had no issues deferring the necessary resources to the task. He recruited the very best people, and unusually in the sector at the time, he focused on project management as a competitive differentiator, with a single person appointed to oversee any particular project from start to completion, across all departments and countries.

Clarke appointed Paul Heugh, now CEO of Skarbek Associates, to lead a central global project management team, and encouraged him to champion project management training throughout the organization. Clarke was so passionate about this that he attended the fundamentals course himself not just once but repeatedly, dropping in whenever he could as the course was rolled out through the organization, so that it was embedded and, in Heugh's words, became 'a part of the DNA of the business' (and a part of every player on the team). It was a new approach, a new way of thinking, and a new execution mindset and capability – and the differentiator, to ensure GSK Consumer Healthcare implemented its strategy better, faster and more efficiently than its competitors.

Bringing together the marketing team and R&D team

In total, some 150 first-class individuals were selected from around the world to staff the Future Group, with offices split between the UK and New Jersey in the US. One of the central strategies of the Future Group was to bring together the marketing team and the R&D team, so they could work together to build platforms for the global brands. This was quite a different approach from the departmental structure that had prevailed before, where people would be grouped under HR, regulatory, R&D, marketing, sales and so on, and sit in an office with other people in the same group as themselves. Tim Wright, who headed up the Future Group commercial team and later stepped into John Clarke's shoes when he was promoted to president, explains how the centralization of the marketing and R&D teams evolved.

In the early days of the Future Group, Wright was invited to run the commercial team for Denture Care, a category newly acquired by Consumer Healthcare and 'not the sort of thing you want to tell your mum you've been promoted to', says Clarke, though potentially it was a goldmine. Wright's counterpart in the R&D department was Stan Lech. Just before the two men began to work together on the project, they looked at a plan of the building where they were to work in New Jersey, and saw that the R&D facility was in one corner of the building while the marketing offices were in a completely different corner. 'It made no sense,' says Wright, 'considering we were trying to build this thing together.'

After about six weeks it became clear that the architecture was indeed a huge impediment; they were in the same building but might as well have been in different cities – and so Stan Lech picked up his laptop and moved to the marketing area of the building, bringing two or three of his senior R&D people with him. 'That was the first time in the company that the department structure had broken down and we were sitting as a part of the brand as opposed to a part of a department,' says Wright, 'but we were still in offices in the traditional sense.'

'Then two things collided,' says Wright. 'One, we were putting more and more people into the building and we didn't have the space for them; and two, a lot of people were in global roles and travelling a lot, and the idea of having all these empty offices was ridiculous – so someone got the idea of moving to open plan.' There would be an area in the building, in this case for Denture Care, where everybody working on the account would gather and work together regardless of his or her department. 'This really rocked the boat of a lot of departments,' says Wright, 'but it was great!' And it didn't stop there. Stan Lech then conjured up the idea of having what he called a 'kitchen table', just like at home, where people might sit around and have natural, spontaneous conversations. 'Stan and I would sit at the kitchen table with our immediate direct reports,' says Wright, 'and then surrounding us would be other tables and desks and little telephone rooms and meeting rooms.' There would be 'no fixed address', so people would walk in every morning with their laptop bag and sit down in a chair of their choice.

The advantages of this new office layout proved extraordinary. A highbrow PhD scientist in R&D, for instance, may never even have considered the marketing of a product; indeed, with the traditional separation of departments, why should she? She would be physically and intellectually separated, focusing only on the science. In the new layout, sitting at the kitchen table, there was no choice but to see the work of the commercial operators as well, and its relevance. The result was that departmental friction was significantly reduced. 'We saw a disappearance of departmental arrogance,' adds Clarke. 'The goal changed from being "I'm smarter than you" to a collective growth target where everybody around the table was going to be a beneficiary.'

A further marked advantage of operating around the kitchen table was the spontaneous meetings, held as and when they were needed around a relevant activity. An issue might arise over a particular formulation, for example. Easy with this new format to say, 'Let's get together; we might need the marketing guy, and better bring in legal, too.' Long gone the days when issues would have to wait for scheduled meetings, and when meetings were attended unnecessarily, as was so often the case in the old system. That precious, non-renewable resource of time was saved, and operations sped up immeasurably.

'We could save weeks at each stage,' says Clarke, 'eliminate a year from a project cycle.' And, he added, 'the potency of this collaborative working showed itself at its best in the creation of ideas. We still had brainstorming management meetings but just as many ideas were generated around the kitchen table where, actually, brainstorming was happening all the time.' Someone might pose a question, for instance, perhaps a question that might not justify an email, or even seem a little stupid and awkward to ask in a more formal setting. 'But you know,' says Wright, 'in stupid questions we found lie the seeds of innovation.'

The model proved so successful in New Jersey that it was replicated by GSK all over the world, in London, Shanghai and India – everywhere kitchen tables were defined by and dedicated to brands such as Panadol, NiQuitin and Sensodyne. Down came banners across the façades of Consumer Healthcare buildings that read *Research & Development Centre*; in their place, the words *Innovation Centre*. After all, that's what the business was about: innovating new products and getting them to market.

Prioritizing/focusing/speeding things up

Brand focus was everything – and the simpler and more focused, the better. In a multinational the size of GSK Consumer Healthcare, there might be 100 plus new initiatives that it plans to launch into numerous countries in several regions around the world; and for each initiative there are multiple functions involved: R&D, marketing, manufacturing and more. It is a hugely complex business, and one that needs to be simplified in order to concentrate effort. Says Paul Heugh, 'Anyone who says that many things are a priority actually means that nothing is a priority at all. The ability to nominate the top priority – the priority above all else – is rare and incredibly valuable.'

In the Future Group, the complex was made simple by selecting the top ten priorities. 'Global business planning would take months,' Heugh explains, 'then one afternoon we'd distil everything on to a single page and put it on a flipchart. Then we'd look for the big numbers.' The theory of big numbers, he explains, is a process of identifying the initiatives that will drive maximum business growth in a given period of time, usually a year; it's a way of focusing effort on the revenue or the trading profit. Prioritization – selecting the top ten objectives, then selecting the most important three on the list to be implemented first – was applied throughout the organization. Accomplishments on the top three objectives could be reviewed on a weekly basis, simultaneously looking forward as well as back – 'this is what we achieved this week', they'd say – thus maintaining a sense of accomplishment as well as momentum to move forward, and breaking down what needed to be achieved day by day.

For the top team in the Future Group – the Performance and Operating Committee – the measurement and visibility of performance and speed of operations was cranked up in a way never seen before. 'I'm not keen on monthly meetings,' Clarke says wryly. With the simple shift from monthly to weekly meeting, Clarke wound up the rhythm of execution and had everyone on their toes.

'He introduced operations meetings every Monday morning,' explains Heugh. 'It didn't matter where you were, in Philadelphia, London or Beijing, in the office, or in a hotel. Monday 1pm GMT and you were on a teleconference call to attend the meeting. There was a lot of resistance at the start but people were won over, it meant everyone knew exactly what was going on,' says Heugh. Every week the same questions were on the agenda: what are the issues and what needs to be communicated? A traffic light system – red, amber and green – was introduced to monitor implementation at every level, something Clarke believed to be critical and very powerful.

'It wasn't easy *not* to do things you said you were going to do,' says Heugh. 'John held you accountable. A note was sent out at the end of each meeting with action points and you knew this would be reviewed at the next meeting. It completely changed the operating structure and rhythm of business. We euphemistically referred to it as "Rome", the building of the empire,' he says, with a smile on his face. The sense of common purpose and energy generated was palpable. 'It wasn't draconian at all,' says Clarke. 'People were proud to display a green light on a Monday morning, and they'd be congratulated. We didn't need to focus on the reds and ambers. Peer pressure and a positive rivalry worked brilliantly.'

Communication/commitment

If Clarke's most defining skill was the distilling of strategy to its simplest message, then a close second was the *communication* of this simplest of messages to the team, again and again, almost to the point of insulting people's intelligence. When he joined the company it was, at best, 'informing people', he says. 'I could see there was lots going on below the surface that nobody knew about.' Clarke changed all this. With his characteristic thoroughness he approached communications as a process unto itself. 'Communication is definitely strategic when you defer the sorts of sums we were spending at both country and global levels to get a result,' he says.

It was the Future Group's job to focus on global brand innovation and equity, but without the regional and country marketing teams, nothing would have been deployed – and communication between the two was critical. Meetings were held throughout the year to plan and disseminate information, but then every year in June, 'we had something called the "Go meeting"', says Wright, 'which was a big global jamboree of Future Group excellence to show people what was going to be the plan for next year, what was going to be launched – and to excite and engage them.' The top 500 people globally would congregate in a smart hotel somewhere in the world: London, New Jersey, New Delhi, it didn't really matter as long as everyone was in the same room. 'It was a huge cost,' says Clarke, 'but crucial.'

Video conferencing has its place, but this first step of the cycle simply had to be face to face. People had to truly understand what the objectives were for the coming year. Researchers would stand up on stage and present their ideas. It was a sort of 'educational download', says Clarke, 'very instructive and motivational'. But importantly, the communication wasn't just one way. 'I've seen companies tell people to launch a particular product,' he says. 'People can find a hundred ways for that to fail. But if people understand it and have skin in the game, the chance of success is much, much higher.' So once the researchers had presented their ideas, everyone in the room had the opportunity to ask questions, make suggestions, and contribute to the bettering of the product. 'The feeling that people had a part in the product was potent,' says Clarke.

Of course, John Clarke had opportunity to present his messages on stage as well – and this he took extremely seriously. Clarke had been involved in advertising both at GSK Consumer Healthcare and in his previous post in Unilever, and clearly found the art of messaging highly enjoyable. 'Communicating to an audience is no different than a TV commercial,' he argues. 'It's all about taking people to the movies, not to read a novel. You lose people with words on PowerPoint.' Clarke's demeanour lightened visibly as he spoke about this, his enthusiasm shone – as if it weren't bright enough already – and my interest peaked as a presenter myself. 'It's about mnemonics,' he says. 'You know the brain doesn't remember anything it's seen before? The message must be vibrant and dramatically different, visual and crisp. I showed a picture of an ice-cream with two blobs on it once, everyone understood.'

No cost was too great or time too precious to perfect the delivery of his message. Clarke employed a coach, a retired CNN news reporter, to hone the delivery of his words that would support the pictures, especially for when the camera was up close on his 'talking head'. 'The audience is looking for sincerity in the eyes and face,' he says, at which point I wondered at the paradox of overworking a delivery to a point where it might come across as more acted than genuine. But this is the art. The message must be crystallized and rehearsed, yet above all it must be believable. For all presenters, whether enthusiasts, born naturals or gibbering jellies, the message must be believable. An audience sniffs out a fake without even realizing it.

'John understood that a message must be communicated simply,' says Paul Heugh, 'but also repetitively, so that people start to internalize it.' Following the annual Go conference, a package would be compiled for the general managers to cascade the message through the 14,000 people in the organization, and there were follow-up internal briefing systems by email on a daily basis. This process wasn't without its challenges. In a matrix organization such as GSK Consumer Healthcare, regional offices had their own objectives to meet as well as the global objectives instructed from above – and priorities and time had to be managed effectively.

Paul Heugh explains, 'The high-level objectives are cascaded top-down throughout the organization; and then the different functions and regions are invited to present their own objectives and these are gathered bottom-up, and an audit carried out to see where they are aligned and where they are not.' And then, as across the company, they are highlighted red, amber or green: red where the global objectives are not appearing but should, amber where the global objectives are not appearing but for a valid reason (for example, a product can't be launched for regulatory reasons), and green where the global objectives are appearing. The message is clear: it is these objectives highlighted in green that are the priority. Global objectives trump regional objectives every time.

Then of course these objectives are to be aligned with each and every individual who is to do the work: not easy when an individual is answerable to both his or her regional or country line manager *and* global team or functional leader. The global project manager, who supported global initiatives, had a remit to go right through all silos across functions and regions of the world, to align and co-ordinate one unified plan.

But where an individual has two bosses, or even three or four bosses depending on the number of projects they're working on, naturally it can create a conflict of interests and put considerable pressure on everyone. The approach to solving this issue wasn't to police it in some sort of draconian manner, but rather to have discussion groups where people could discuss their objectives and self-direct the alignment of their objectives to the global objectives, as well as the functional and regional ones closer to hand. 'It sounds simple but there could be a degree of resistance,' says Heugh. 'People didn't necessarily like to be chased to complete objectives to a deadline from afar, but they could see that it worked and respected the process.' The process allowed individuals to write their own annual objectives on which they would be evaluated at the end of the year. The bonus structure was kept simple: 50 per cent allocated on team results, measurable from sales in any one year, and 50 per cent allocated on individual contribution.

'It probably took a couple of years to adapt to the new global way of working,' says Heugh, after which Clarke rose to the top position of President of Consumer Healthcare. In his place as head of the Future Group was appointed one of the world's leading marketers from within the company, Tim Wright. 'In those first couple of years the organization was still evolving,' says Wright. 'It wasn't until John was in the top position that there was a universal, blinded commitment to the model.'

It was this total commitment that was, in Tim Wright's view, the key to success. 'I have seen the same structure fail in so many companies,' he says, 'and I believe it is entirely related to the conviction and commitment of the leadership.' And by this he means not only John Clarke, as president of the company, but also the regional presidents – in Europe, the US and the rest of the world – who are tasked with implementing the strategy across the world.

'It didn't matter how smart my team was in the Future Group,' says Wright, 'it was the regional presidents who were required to make it clear to the general managers, who would make it clear to the local marketers, regulatory people and salespeople, that this was the way to go. Their reputations, their salaries, their bonuses and careers were resting on this stuff working, and if they weren't prepared to back us in a visual and vocal way, then nothing would happen. Gaining the commitment of the people is nine tenths of the game,' he says. 'If they're not committed then you have to be calling them every single week to see what's going on; if they are committed, then you don't.'

There were several factors that Wright believes contributed to the successful buy-in of regional presidents and their teams across the world. Conviction and commitment of the leadership has already been mentioned, but it is worthy of emphasis that Wright believes Clarke was utterly convinced that the *only* route to doubling growth figures was through improved marketing, R&D and advertising, and that this could only be achieved through running it with single-minded precision at the centre.

Secondly, the company's financial model was changed to reflect the shift in strategy. It moved from 'country' profit and loss accounts to 'brand' profit and loss accounts, which, says Wright, 'sent a message to the whole company that we were about building global brands'. Thirdly, there was a seriousness attached to Clarke's recruitment of staff. 'In a lot of organizations, the people brought into central roles are tired, worn-out marketers,' says Wright, 'but Clarke did it very differently. He brought in people who had been successful general managers so they already had leadership credentials. People knew who they were.' And fourth, these general managers were well funded. There is no point having great people in roles if they don't have the money to do the work.

Finally, Clarke was very clear about the objectives of both central and regional management. Central management was responsible for the global strategies, and the local management was responsible for executing these strategies in their regions. He says, 'We cascaded elements of the management objective list through the company, and I think we did that very well.' These collective elements led to a mutual respect between the leadership of the Future Group and the leadership of the regions, and the results were shown in the numbers.

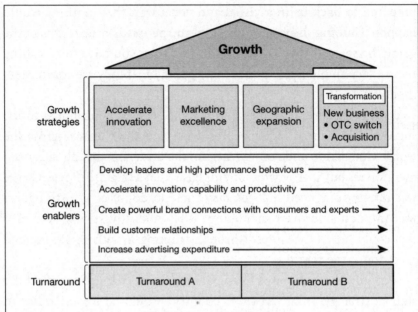

Clarke's Growth Cathedral

Clarke's brilliance was to distil a strategy to its simplest form. In a single word, his objective was 'growth': the aim to be the fastest-growing healthcare company in the world. Clearly this single objective had to be broken down, but the strategies to achieving this growth were equally clear: accelerated innovation, marketing excellence, geographic expansion and new business. These four growth strategies answered the question *why would GSK Consumer Healthcare win?* The next question asked was *how would these strategies be enabled?* This was thought through with exacting care, the answers spelled out in order: developing leaders and high performance behaviours; the acceleration of innovation capability and productivity; the creation of powerful brand connections with consumers and experts; building customer relationships, and so on. Note, too, at the bottom of the cathedral, two aspects of the business were underperforming and growth could only be achieved if these failing businesses were turned around.

Implementing unpopular strategies: A cost reduction programme

What happens in a company when a strategy is highly unpopular? For example, say the words 'cost reduction' or 'restructuring' and blood will run cold, and cynicism and negativity will rise. Here we look briefly at how a potentially deeply unpopular and negative strategy can be executed with great success.

When first taking on the role of President of GSK Consumer Healthcare, the uncomfortable truth is that Clarke had inherited a company that had allowed itself to become complacent; the drawing of profit had taken priority over reinvestment in R&D, and advertising and promotions support for the company's brands had eroded to dangerously uncompetitive levels. This had to change. Money was needed to boost advertising and promotion and R&D, and there was no illusion that there would be a magic cash injection from the parent company; the monies needed would have to come from within the company's own cost structure.

As with everything that Clarke touched, his approach was thorough; the global cost-saving and efficiency programme required was regarded as a strategy unto itself, and a team was put in place with a clear target to save £100m within three years, equivalent to 6 per cent of non-advertising and promotion costs. To endow the project with the seriousness it deserved, and to ensure maximum impact and engagement across the organization, an experienced general manager and member of the company's senior leadership team, Simon Pulsford, was appointed to lead the project, reporting directly to the CEO.

The genius of this project was in its communications. Mention cost cutting and what are the first thoughts that usually come to mind? Job losses, insecurity and austerity? 'This doesn't have to be the case,' says Simon Pulsford, who magnificently turned what might have been regarded as a negative into a positive, and communicated it to employees in a way that they immediately bought into the idea.

'One of the critical success factors,' he says, 'was to communicate to the business that although a cost-saving programme, Project Rainbow would be positive for the business and positive for the people in the business. It was made very clear there would be no cutting of costs in areas of the business that were critical for growth. Rather costs would be cut by the reduction of complexity, for example, and the resultant savings would be redirected to advertising and promotion in order to drive growth.'

To illustrate the point, Simon invited employees from around the world to send packs of Panadol (GSK's paracetamol) from their respective countries, which were then displayed on a single table at the launch of this global cost-saving and efficiency programme. There were Panadol packages in different colours, with different wording and different logos, of different sizes, containing 6 or 12 or 24 tablets, made of different formulations depending on their country of origin. Each type of Panadol package, however marginal the difference between it and another package, is recorded in the business as a different Stock Keeping Unit, or SKU. The greater the number of SKUs, the greater the complexity – in both the factory and in purchasing.

With Panadol, as it turned out to be the case with many of the company's products, there was an enormous number of variations that had mutated and evolved in random Darwinian fashion, going unnoticed and unchecked. Only when the array of different Panadol boxes from around the world was laid on the table for everyone to see, was it clear the scale of the complexity – and the scale of the opportunity. The complexity didn't add value to the brand; quite the opposite. If it could be simplified with fewer formulations and aligned packaging across the world, the resulting economies of scale would be massive.

People understood this immediately. For many companies, a cost-saving exercise would be just that: an exercise to save money. GSK Consumer Healthcare was in the relatively privileged position to be able to say to its staff, 'every penny you save, you can spend'. And it was also made very clear that every member of staff would benefit personally, through bonuses, as a result of growth and increased sales in any one year, and as a direct result of their individual contribution to reducing costs.

Still, though easy in concept, it wasn't an easy programme to implement – which made communication all the more critical. It was important that John Clarke's message was clear: that this cost-saving and efficiency drive was a priority, not just a nice-to-do; that it was at the heart of how they were going to conduct business.

Typically, Clarke didn't skimp on the necessary support to put the strategy into action. A central Rainbow project management team was set up, with Simon Pulsford at its head and two financial professionals at its centre to provide governance, analysis and monitoring support. Dedicated people were appointed in key functions across the organization: supply chain, R&D, global marketing, procurement, IT and communications. And each of the three geographical regions – North America, Europe and International – was also appointed a dedicated representative to drive the project.

'The first step was to ascertain what were the costs throughout the organization,' says Pulsford. This involved a data collecting exercise of massive proportions. Perhaps unsurprisingly, many companies don't have a clear handle on their costs and GSK Consumer Healthcare was no exception. The reality is that through various mergers, acquisitions and developments through the years, there can be a resulting 'dog's dinner' of financial practices in place, just as there was an overwhelming array of formulations and packaging for the same product. Financial data was gathered across the organization, in every function and every region across the globe. Likewise, SKU and formulation data was gathered for every brand.

Once the data gathering had been completed, it was then possible to identify areas in which costs could be saved – the most obvious areas being the reduction of SKUs and associated raw materials, and the standardization of packaging, as well as the more complex challenges such as restructuring, third party alliances and the simplification of processes. Realistic targets were put in place and people were expected to deliver.

'If you took your foot off the gas, the process would grind to a halt immediately,' says Pulsford, 'but the level of commitment from the senior management team was consistent throughout the life of the programme.' There was a rhythm and discipline in the execution, and without fail, the communication was crystal clear. Top management didn't dictate what to do; it just set clear overall targets and parameters that were realistic, and provided the resources to enable people to get on with the job. There was no micro-managing. 'From the CEO at the top,' explains Pulsford, 'you could look down a clear tube right through the organization. There was total alignment. No diversion from the objectives.'

It was the project team's job to co-ordinate the work of the various stakeholders and to ensure the agreed plans were implemented, and importantly, to ensure the business was kept well informed of the progress against the targets. Communication was a constant, with bulletins sent out monthly and more frequently when important messages needed to be conveyed. And crucially, the project team's communication wasn't just switched to transmit; it was very much open to 'receive' as well.

People would feedback their success stories – where and how money had been saved – and these stories, often imaginative, invariably motivating, would then be celebrated and shared with the rest of the organization. Everyone knew exactly how much money had been saved and how this exact sum of money had been spent on advertising and promotion in order to grow the business. People shared ideas, replicated ideas in different functions and different countries, and were constantly invited to pitch in with new suggestions for further cost reductions – and these in turn were shared and replicated through the organization. Thus the Rainbow project wasn't just theoretical; it became demonstrable. People could witness, share and become beneficiaries of the business growth. They were a living, breathing part of the growth, and success fed upon success.

The result was the generation of millions of pounds, sustained over years. The original target of saving £100m in three years was met, and in six years, this figure was more than doubled with over £250m saved. These savings were reinvested into increased advertising and promotion, which rose by 3 per cent of sales in the first three years and more thereafter. Sales growth increased from 2 per cent to over 6 per cent, and the company achieved its objective of becoming the fastest growing company in its sector. And, while recognizing the multifaceted nature of executing the strategy, the critical factor for success was, in Pulsford's view, communications: the turning of a potentially negative message into a positive, and a constant two-way flow of information to share, celebrate and reinforce the company's objectives and the importance of everybody's contributions to its achievements.

CHAPTER TEN

The Challenges and Successes – Making Diversity Happen

I am only one, but I am one. I cannot do everything, but I can do something. And I will not let what I cannot do interfere with what I can do.

Edward Everett Hale, American author, historian
and Unitarian minister

Making a diversity strategy happen

The last few decades have seen a massive cultural shift in what might loosely be called diversity and inclusion in the workplace – and it isn't only about equal and fair representation; there is a strong business case for it too. The diversity of thinking brought to the table by people of different backgrounds, education and experience, observing the world through different lenses, is thought to lead to better decision-making, innovation and very often better bottom line results. Diversity and inclusion in the workplace is about understanding and valuing people of different races, ethnicities, ages, religions, disabilities and sexual orientation. But here we look at one very large group comprising half the world's population that, in a number of arenas, still falls under the 'diversity' headline: women. One woman who has single-handedly had a huge impact on the inclusion of women in the traditionally male-dominated world of British company boards is financier and campaigner Dame Helena Morrissey, appointed Commander of the

Order of the British Empire in the 2012 New Year Honours for services to business, and promoted to Dame Commander of the Order of the British Empire (DBE) in the 2017 Birthday Honours for services to diversity in financial services.

While it may be difficult to understand how anything other than equal opportunity makes sense in the workplace and the world in general, not many of us have dedicated our lives to achieving this – yet Dame Helena Morrissey has made it her life's work. She quotes Indian Hindu monk Swami Vivekananda, who said, 'Take one idea. Make that one idea your life, think of it, dream of it, live on that idea. Let the brain, muscles, nerves, every part of your body, be full of that idea and just leave every other idea alone. This is the way to success.'

Morrissey's 'idea' – which, she says, has made the difference between having a successful business career in the eyes of others and actually feeling confident that she is making a valuable contribution – is the big rebalance between men and women, something she says has ramifications for her family, for her roles in business, for the commentary and analysis and speeches she makes, and which is indeed the motivation for the writing of her recent book, *A Good Time to be a Girl*. She acknowledges that the idea is far from new, but nonetheless feels people don't fully understand just how powerful genuine balancing would be, and that her contribution is to try and change that.

Inspiration/motivation for addressing gender imbalance

Three fundamental factors have shaped her passion. The first was her early childhood. 'I was motivated to a large degree by my grandmothers,' she says. 'Both highly intelligent women who were top of their class at school and yet didn't go to university, because of the class they were born into and the time that it was. They had amazing talent and weren't fulfilled in the way they should have been, for their own sake as well as for society – and that made me sad.'

Then Morrissey was shocked to find her own career progression curtailed, as late as the early 1990s. She was 26 years old at the time, working as a fund manager at a prestigious City firm in London, and was passed over for promotion after returning to work from maternity leave, the reason given, 'there's just some doubt over your commitment with a baby'. Her first child is now 27 but she still visibly struggles with the injustice of it, not blaming her employers but the attitude that prevailed in the City at the time. Morrissey's two male counterparts received promotion and she assumed she had been denied this because of a failing in her performance, but no, 'your work is great', she was told. It was just the commitment thing – though clearly this is something Morrissey has in spades.

The third reason was – and continues to be – young women approaching her and asking how she manages to combine career and family. And no wonder: she is famously the mother of nine children, her husband opting mid-career to stay at home and look after their growing brood. 'I wanted to help them [women] avoid some of the things that I recognize I had done myself,' she says. 'I had tried to lean in to the status quo and work harder and be like the men, but then realized I was much better at my job when I could just be myself,' she says.

Becoming CEO of Newton

When Morrissey was passed over for promotion, she was at first confused and disappointed – but then she says she had a moment of clarity: she couldn't change the existing environment, so she made it her job to find a new one. She applied for a job as number two (of two) on the bond desk of a smaller, less well-known firm in the City called Newton Investment Management. It was a junior role in a relatively backwater area for the company – on the face of it a less promising situation than the job from which she had resigned, but its inclusive culture was to make all the difference. 'Newton was way ahead of its time,' she says, 'embracing diversity of thought long before diversity was a word in business.' At Newton, her commitment was valued and within seven years, following a takeover of the company, she was appointed CEO. Another 15 years and she and her colleagues had developed a number of market-leading strategies and grown assets under management from £20bn to over £50bn.

So how did she rise to the position of chief executive so quickly and oversee the doubling of assets in 15 years? First, she says, 'a moment of disruption was my great opportunity'. Her career had been progressing well at Newton, but the opportunity to become chief executive at the age of 35, with no business experience or management training to her name, was unexpected – most of all by her. She had actually wanted to be appointed chief investment officer (CIO) and, as one of a four-strong Investment Strategy group, felt that she was well positioned as a candidate when the American Mellon Bank took over Newton and there was some movement among members of the management team. Mellon's UK-based chief actually offered her the CIO role, but then one of her colleagues stopped by her desk and quietly told her that the other senior investors weren't keen – the reason being they felt it important for the CIO to have an equities background since most of the firm's assets were invested in the stock market. And here was the surprise – instead, they would like her to be CEO.

Morrissey reflects on this extraordinary day in her life, confessing that she honestly didn't know what being CEO entailed. But what she did know was that she believed in Newton and what it had to offer its clients, she believed in the team and in her ability to lead – and that it was a rare, perhaps once-in-a-lifetime opportunity. In the spirit of boldness that she and her six daughters regularly chant when one or other of them might be dithering, she 'leapt before she looked' – and didn't glance back.

Her early days as CEO were a steep learning curve with multiple moments of self-doubt but, she argues, she emerged on the other side older, wiser and just possibly better at her job than if she had taken a more conventional route to get there, if only because she had to learn so quickly.

On reflection there were a few good calls in those early days that led to the company's success. The first, focus – critical in the effective implementation of strategy. Morrissey shut out the siren voices calling her to reinvent Newton and develop new strategies that weren't core to its strengths. 'I had learned – in life as well as at work – that we cannot always please everyone and that it's a mistake even to try,' she says. 'In business, the key is to offer *something* of value to some people; in life, to know what matters to you, a framework for the myriad decisions each of us need to take.' Morrissey understood that after the takeover it was more important than ever to focus on what they did best, to ensure their clients were being well served and had confidence in their continuing performance.

Having said this, they weren't static – the marketplace was changing around them and to stick rigidly to what had worked in the past and not to evolve their investment services would have been suicidal. So secondly, they actively sought opportunity from change.

And thirdly, Morrissey nurtured the culture that had been so central to the business since it had been founded. A takeover is inevitably dislocating, and one of the reasons she believes her colleagues backed her as CEO was because of her collaborative style of leadership, which enabled employees to contribute to the vision of the future. 'I felt this acutely as Newton's new CEO,' she says. 'One minute I was one of many fund managers, the next I was officially the boss, but not in a position to *instruct* my colleagues. Instead my role was to lead by influencing them, having first listened to what was on their minds, then to form a plan that took account of their views – or explain why I was going in a different direction – and bring them with me.' Morrissey explains this approach was partly the result of the circumstances of her appointment, but also a feature of active investment management firms, in which investors often view themselves as self-employable. 'The CEO is more akin to the conductor of an orchestra than a prima donna,' she says, adding that this leadership model is becoming reality for many other industries, and in politics too. 'People will no longer be told what to do by leaders who don't connect with them,' she says.

The company was undeniably successful under Morrissey's leadership, but would have been nothing without the right team. 'No one has a monopoly on great ideas' is Newton's motto, and Morrissey and her colleagues made a deliberate effort to develop diversity of thought and perspective. As with all teams, 'the best investment teams are not necessarily groups of the most qualified individuals', she says. 'The interaction between team members plays a vital role.'

However, the diversity of thought and perspective was necessarily constrained, as it was in the rest of the fund management industry, by one very obvious fact: with the odd exception, the players in the team were men. With the very few young women in the industry continuing to approach her for advice, Morrissey decided that it was high time that she did something about it.

First attempts to get more women into senior positions

Her first step in 2005, backed by her Boston-based boss Ron O'Hanley, was to launch a women's initiative for the parent company's European businesses. Like a number of gender diversity efforts at the time, it centred on networking events, often involving a talk by a high-profile woman that was inspiring but sadly not inspiring enough to actually effect any change. And so this continued for three or four years, with lots of networking but no advancement in the representation of women at senior levels, to the point that Morrissey nearly gave up – until she realized that others were struggling in isolation as well. In 2009, she was invited to give a talk herself at Goldman Sachs, as part of its 2009 Diversity Week. Afterwards she took part in a discussion with a number of people from different organizations who shared their efforts, and their frustrations, in encouraging women into more senior roles. One of the attendees was Baroness Mary Goudie, a Labour peer – and together they agreed that they wanted to do something to break the deadlock. Clearly, they needed to take a completely different approach.

As Morrissey started to research the subject, she learned that Deutsche Telekom was making an effort to ensure there were at least 30 per cent women at all levels of seniority. She liked the specific, numeric target, and recognized they had made a mistake in not setting clear goals; she realized the importance of measuring and tracking progress just as one would a business objective – and she liked the actual percentage: 30 per cent. From her own experience, it felt that 30 per cent was the minimum threshold at which she stopped feeling like a minority. If she was the only woman in the room, which was all too frequently the case, she sometimes felt self-conscious and would only intervene after careful thought, while if she was one woman of three in a group of ten, she was just another person in the room and felt confident to speak freely.

She was impressed, too, by the way in which Deutsche Telekom was promoting its ambition. The company's then chief executive, René Obermann, was clear in his message: 'Taking on more women in management positions is not about the enforcement of misconstrued egalitarianism,' he said. 'Having a greater number of women at the top will quite simply enable us to operate better.' His statement was striking in deliberately distancing the movement away from political correctness and toward the business case, but it also had gravitas in that it was spoken by a person in a position of power.

This led Morrissey to a further realization. To date, women's initiatives had largely been about women talking to women about women's issues. This is a recipe for going nowhere; it is an impossible task to expect an under-represented group to solve the problem of its own under-representation. Women in such groups might help each other feel less alone, but in order to succeed in enrolling more women into senior positions, to open doors that might otherwise be closed, then leaders in positions of power and influence – which at this time were mostly men – needed to be on board.

Morrissey was playing with these thoughts, sharing ideas with Baroness Mary Goudie and other senior businesswomen in an attempt to create some sort of an action plan, when an opportunity arose – one that rippled from the cataclysmic dislocation of the global financial crisis of 2008 and was (Morrissey would be the first to admit) outside their sphere of control yet nonetheless extremely beneficial to their cause. They needed a vision, and as the wreckage of the financial collapse was analysed, it seemed obvious with the benefit of hindsight that there was an inherent flaw in the boards and management teams of banks being comprised almost exclusively of white, middle-class, middle-aged, affluent men. They might be brilliant, but cut from the same cloth they were far more likely to back one another's opinions than to challenge them. By early 2010, the realization was growing that the boardroom – described by former fund manager Lord Myners as a 'retirement home for the great and the good'– needed a shake-up. The door was ajar for different 'types' to become directors, and an obvious place to start was to address the scarcity of women on boards.

In 2008, fewer than 12 per cent of the directors at the UK's top 100 listed companies were women. Cast a broader net and the representation of women on the boards of the top 250 UK listed companies, the FTSE 250, was just 7 per cent. Besides the obvious risk of groupthink, 93 per cent men is clearly unrepresentative of society and just about any company's customer base.

Ambition and action, founding the 30% Club

Morrissey recognized the opportunity to ride the zeitgeist and chose to act, despite what had been something of a lukewarm response when she and Dame Mary Goudie had invited some 40 senior businesswomen to lunch to solicit input into their emerging idea a little while before. This time she invited just 14 women to lunch – those who had shown enthusiasm – and suggested the specific idea of the 30% Club. Together they agreed on a simple, narrow but ambitious goal: to reach 30 per cent women on UK company boards over the following five years through voluntary, business-led change.

It was clear the members of this 30% Club needed to be chairs of boards, since the boards were *their* boards and they had the authority to change things. Naturally these chairs of boards were almost exclusively chair*men* of boards – at the time there was only a single FTSE 100 company, Land Securities, that had a female chair: Dame Alison Carnwath. Dame Carnwath was a fantastic supporter of the 30% Club, but nonetheless, there was only one of her.

That very same afternoon, Morrissey tested out the 30% Club idea on two highly regarded and prominent FTSE 100 chairmen: Sir Roger Carr, then chairman of Centrica, and Sir Win Bischoff, then chairman of Lloyds Bank. Would they support a campaign to reach 30 per cent women on boards within five years? Both jumped at the opportunity. In their words, 'When we have women on our boards, the dynamic is better, the decision-making is better – but there are too few of them.'

The endorsement and the evangelism of these two captains of industry transformed the thinking around the issue. If there had been a degree of scepticism at the start, this was quickly blown away. The scarcity of women in senior positions was no longer a women's issue but a business issue – and men and women were going to work together to resolve it.

The approach taken by the 30% Club, says Morrissey, was very much to think big, start small but start now. 'If you have a compelling vision, actually people find it very difficult to say no,' says Morrissey. She admits that the route to their ambition was somewhat vague at the start, rather like 'driving through fog', but nothing had worked before so they needed to draw up a new map to reach their destination. 'We were wholly open to fresh ideas,' says Morrissey. 'We listened and adapted quickly as we made progress or encountered setbacks. I became a great believer in pilots to test ideas quickly rather than endless theorizing. After all, we knew we *had* to experiment to make progress.'

As it turned out, despite the odd wobble, the 30% Club caught the mood of the moment; the financial crisis created real appetite for change, and rather faster than Morrissey expected. The 30% Club was officially launched with seven founding chair supporters in 2010, but what Morrissey hadn't factored in was that the supporters were all very competitive with each other. 'Suddenly everybody wanted to recruit more chair supporters to the club than the next guy, and we went from seven to over 200 chair supporters in fairly short order!'

Then in February 2011, a few months after the 30% Club launch, Lord Davies, who had been invited to examine the scarcity of women on UK company boards, published his cross-party public review. Like the 30% Club, the review addressed the lack of gender diversity on British boards as a key business issue at a time when it was still being narrowly boxed by many as an equalities, diversity or women's issue. It emphasized the added value of diverse perspectives, economic arguments on talent management and the modernizing of British business, global credibility, impact on reputation and the stability of the economy – and, like the 30% Club, it backed voluntary action rather than mandatory quotas.

Over the next five years, the Davies Steering Committee and the 30% Club formed a powerful double-act, combining supportive public policy with private sector action. By the end of 2015 – the self-imposed deadline for both parties – the percentage number of FTSE 100 board positions held by women had risen to 26 per cent – just above Lord Davies' goal of 25 per cent and a little short of Morrissey's goal of 30 per cent. Still, it was a big leap from the 12 per cent figure that had held for so many years previously, and what's more, there were no longer any exclusively male FTSE 100 boards. The FTSE 250 companies achieved even more progress from their weaker starting position: nearly 20 per cent female directors and just 15 all-male boards remaining.

And time hasn't eroded this advancement: quite the opposite. The 30% Club eventually reached its target and in January 2021 women held 30.7 per cent of FTSE 100 board positions, and the business case is even stronger as chairs report on the positive impact that women are having at the top table, changing the nature of the discussion and level of challenge, and improving the performance of the board all round. Few British business leaders now ask why we need more women in senior positions; instead, energies are now focused on how to get women into leadership positions and how to sustain the change.

Meanwhile, the initial aim of the 30% Club has broadened, both geographically and to different stages of women's career paths. Gender inequality is a global phenomenon; the management consulting firm McKinsey estimates that $28tn could be added to the world economy by 2025 if women were to be equal participants in the labour force with men. As of 2021, in an effort to achieve parity for women across the world, the 30% Club set up 16 international chapters, in the US, Canada, Hong Kong, Italy, East Africa, Southern Africa, Australia, Ireland, Turkey, Malaysia, Middle East and North Africa, Brazil, Chile, Colombia, Mexico and Japan. And in the UK and US, the 30% Club developed a cross-company mentoring scheme to support women, usually mid-career, to help build the pipeline of women coming up through the ranks to become the future leaders in some of the world's biggest organizations. 'It is one of the things I am most proud about in terms of what the 30% Club has achieved,' says Morrissey, 'because it's got scale.' Since its inception in 2014, it has supported over 9,000 mentors and mentees from some 200 organizations across more than 30 sectors – and in 2020 it incorporated a global remote mentoring opportunity as well. In the same year, it also increased its aspirations to reach beyond gender and extended its cross-company mentoring programme to include individuals from all under-represented minority groups.

Why the 30% Club succeeded

Morrissey is the first to point to the wave of shifting opinion following the financial crisis of 2008, 'but it wasn't just the zeitgeist or the combination of voices that made an impact', she says. 'The 30% Club's tactics were different to anything that had been tried before – in some respects deliberately so, in others more a stroke of luck.' Through both the campaign's successes and failures, Morrissey learned a lot about how to effect change, which she believes is a replicable formula that can help to achieve the 30% Club's bigger ambition of gender equality. In summary there are five success factors, already touched on: seize the opportunity created by dislocation; focus on the business aspects rather than 'merely' the fairness issue; have a measurable goal with a deadline to create urgency; involve men with the ability to change things; and be open to new ideas.

There was a sixth success factor as well: confidence. There was something of the 'fake it till we make it' about it. 'The 30% Club took one step forward, but we would act as if we had taken two,' says Morrissey. 'We talked up the progress, we celebrated good stories, we were confident. This did not always come easily. But I could see that people wanted to become part of a successful movement and that there was a circularity to that success. The more progress we made, the more progress we were likely to continue making.'

What was intriguing, Morrissey explains, was that 'the bolder I became in my requests, the more likely the response was to be yes'. She cites one particularly ambitious event: a Washington DC breakfast following the launch of the 30% Club chapter in the US, hosted by KPMG, and deliberately planned to coincide with the 2014 IMF conference. It was understood that Mark Carney, Governor of the Bank of England, would be attending the conference, and Morrissey immediately saw this as an opportunity to raise the global profile of the 30% Club. Maybe he could be persuaded to speak at their breakfast?

The answer was encouraging but noncommittal; the Governor's office said that he was minded to accept – if he was free. This wasn't exactly the answer Morrissey was hoping for; she wanted to encourage global bank chiefs to attend the breakfast and knew they would be far more likely to do so if the guest speaker was the Governor of the Bank of England. But she wasn't deterred. She spent a week of her family holiday sending handwritten invitations to CEOs and policymakers, indicating that they *expected* the Governor to be the speaker – meanwhile keeping the Governor's office up to speed with the list of *expected* influential attendees in order to put on the pressure. Brenda Trenowden of ANZ Bank, who later took on the mantle of leading the 30% Club, worked tirelessly to round up the acceptances and, finally, it was confirmed that the Governor would speak. The room was brimming with influential men and women and Carney spoke eloquently about the Bank's 300-year traditions and the importance of diversity in creating a modern culture. The microphone was handed around the room and the CEOs of banks took turns to contribute their own ideas on how to accelerate progress around the world, exactly as Morrissey had envisioned it.

The 30% Club's final key to success was taking what Morrissey describes as a 'feminine' approach to solving a business problem. She understands that the very use of the word 'feminine' is contentious. 'Some object to the very idea that there are characteristics more generally associated with girls and women,' she says. 'Of course, there can be as much, or more, difference between individuals of the same gender as between the genders. That is, in my view, perfectly compatible with using the words "feminine" or "masculine" to describe traits more *commonly* found in either girls or boys. It certainly doesn't mean that those words apply to every *individual* girl or boy.' She understands, too, that there are some who believe the use of the word 'feminine' only perpetuates gender inequalities, but Morrissey believes the opposite to be true. 'If we understand each other's [average] differences better, we can develop more "gender intelligent" strategies to encourage both men and women to thrive, rather than to try to force everyone into a system that tends to motivate one or the other. It's important to recognize that we can be equal but different if we're really going to achieve progress.'

But perhaps the most important point is that the 30% Club wasn't looking to assume the traits of the group it was aiming to join; it didn't aim to simply replace a few men with women assuming the traits of men. That would rather defeat the point. The business case was, and continues to be, about *more* diversity of thought, approaches and behaviours. Thus the 30% Club emphasized rather than diminished the different qualities that women can bring to the table.

One of the most obvious manifestations of this feminine approach was the encouragement of voluntary action rather than legislation or quotas to achieve the goal of more women on boards. In Morrissey's view, 'forcing people to do something would have completely undermined what we were trying to do. Quotas are very much command-and-control, a confrontational rather than an empathetic approach. Few people seem to understand this, focusing on the speed of attaining results, not what those results really signified. The 30% Club's ambitious goal was that men and women would become unified in *desiring* boards with a better gender balance, and that this would help improve culture throughout their organizations, as well as increasing the numbers of women on boards. We wanted to ensure not only that the very best people serve on boards, but to open up the definition of "best" so it did not mean "just like the existing directors".

By partnering not just with the Davies Committee but also with many others who were already doing great work in this area, the 30% Club helped to provide cohesion to fragmented efforts, as well as filling in some gaps, and it created a ripple effect, gradually widening out its radius of influence. Importantly, it had great support in the media. Heather McGregor, Dean of Edinburgh Business School, and Mrs Moneypenny of the *Financial Times* (who was also a member of the 30% Club Steering Committee) were firmly and consistently behind the campaign, amplifying its voice. There were numerous intensive research projects conducted on a pro bono basis, and there was also a broader pro bono publicity campaign masterminded by another member of the Steering Committee, Gay Collins. 'It was incredible how determination and dedication could achieve so much,' says Morrissey, 'with no money changing hands.'

Without being especially conscious of it at the start, Morrissey and her team drew people toward them who had authority and an ability to implement change. 'If they came to think of it as their own idea, so much the better,' says Morrissey. 'I discovered a new power of persuasion in myself, intensified by strong allies.' A number of years after the launch, Sir Win Bischoff, one of the original supporters, spoke of Morrissey's tactics at a dinner in New York: 'Without us realizing what Helena was doing, she was getting us to do the work,' he said, with a broad smile. And Robert Swannell, then chairman of Marks & Spencer, kept up the pressure by stating frequently that he would rather have joined a 50% Club. 'It is a sign of confidence and strength now for men to support gender equality,' says Morrissey. 'We should extend our hand to them, to work with men in power today to create a world where that power is shared.'

Looking at the success of the 30% Club, it's obvious to think of other minority groups as well. Wouldn't they, too, benefit from such an approach? It is encouraging that the 30% Club, while clear that gender has been its starting point and remains a priority, is embracing other under-represented groups. As well as extending its mentoring programme, it has stated clearly that it would like to see one person of colour on every FTSE 350 board – ideally, half of them women of colour. It fully embraces that considerations of ethnicity, disability, sexual orientation, socioeconomic background and beyond are all part of the journey, and believes that only those organizations that foster truly inclusive cultures – cultures that embrace people who look, act and, importantly *think*, different – can fully reach their potential and implement the greatest positive change for their people, their markets and their communities. And to be clear, the 30% Club doesn't regard 30% as a ceiling, but rather as a minimum threshold to stop women being a minority. Once that's achieved, the hope is that there will be momentum to achieve parity.

CHAPTER ELEVEN

Executing Strategy Today and Tomorrow – Mission to the Moon, Mars and Beyond

Far better it is to dare mighty things, to win glorious triumphs, even though checkered by failure, than to rank with those poor spirits who neither enjoy nor suffer much, because they live in the gray twilight that knows neither victory nor defeat.

Theodore Roosevelt, 26th president of the United States, 1901–1909

The National Aeronautics and Space Administration (NASA) plans to send a man and woman to the moon, and build a long-term lunar presence by the end of the 2020s. Not as an end point, but as a stepping stone to prepare and propel humankind to Mars, and beyond. This lunar exploration programme, called Artemis (in Greek mythology Artemis was the daughter of Zeus and Leto, twin sister of Apollo, and Goddess of the Moon), is an extraordinarily bold ambition with a strategy that is being executed in the moment. The journey is happening now, and although it stretches the cognitive ability of those of us watching it unfold, it is in many ways inevitable – our destiny, some would say – as it was for our ancestors to walk from the Rift Valley in Africa and populate the world. Our descendants didn't stop in territories that could easily sustain life, but rather they pushed the boundaries to the more hostile extremities of our planet. In more recent times, explorers risked all, some paying the ultimate price, to reach the most inaccessible places on our planet: north and south poles, the highest point on Earth, and the lowest point, in the deepest ocean. Now, the Artemis generation is breaking bonds with Earth's orbit to explore space.

It has been over fifty years since, on 20 July 1969, the Apollo programme delivered Neil Armstrong and Buzz Aldrin to the moon, and in the decades since, robotic exploration of space has seen huge technological advancements and many new scientific discoveries. Since the year 2000, people have continuously lived and worked aboard the International Space Station 250 miles above Earth, in preparation for venturing further into the solar system.

Strategy – ends, ways and means

In the introduction of this book, we looked at the Apollo programme as an illustration of how a complex challenge might be distilled to a remarkably simple formula that connects 'the end' (namely, the goal) with the 'ways and means' of achieving 'the end', from which a strategy can be deduced. The formula invites the strategist to ensure the appropriate *means* are available to achieve the *ends* (or goals), with the *ways* being the path connecting them.

There can be few finer examples of an audacious and crystal-clear goal than to put the first ever human being on the Moon. Crucially, there was a deadline – the US president of the time, John F Kennedy, declared 'before this decade is out' – with the added urgency to pre-empt the Soviet Union in the space race, thus ingraining the supremacy of democratic freedom over communism.

Today, with the Cold War long over, the urgency is less intense. In the 1960s, there was a degree of risk that was considered acceptable in order to meet the goal, whereas now we are more risk averse, and the life of both the astronauts and those working on the ground is paramount. Nonetheless, the goal is just as clear and even bolder: to send people to the Moon, a distance of 250,000 miles, and then, astonishingly, 140 million miles to the red planet, Mars – with a view to go beyond, to enable human expansion across the solar system and to bring back to Earth new knowledge and opportunities. NASA has been fine-tuning the plan to achieve this vision since then-president Donald Trump called on the agency to lead a human return to the Moon, and beyond, in December 2017. Two years later, he challenged NASA again, this time to send the first woman and next man to the Moon within five years, by 2024. In a move that has been welcomed by the space community, the new administration under President Biden provided an early and clear statement of support for the Artemis programme, although tending to realism over aspiration on timeframes. As of April 2021, there was speculation that the 2024 landing date might be overly ambitious, but the commitment to land as soon as feasibly possible continues, while simultaneously working toward sustainable lunar exploration in the mid-to-late 2020s. It is expected that several years will then be needed orbiting the Moon and on the Moon's surface, to build operational confidence for supporting life and conducting long-term work away from Earth, before embarking on the first multi-year human mission to Mars. The United States is leading in space exploration now, but NASA is acutely aware that as more countries and companies take aim at the Moon, America needs the earliest possible landing to maintain and build on its lead, as well as to prepare for a historic first human mission to Mars.

In the 1960s, the 'means' to undertake the challenge to put man on the Moon was money from the public purse. Such was the importance attached to the mission that John F Kennedy reached out to Congress for funds above and beyond the increases asked for earlier space activities. NASA was the governing and co-ordinating mechanism that would make it happen.

Likewise, NASA is the governing and co-ordinating mechanism for the Artemis programme, and the money is from the public purse – although the tap might not be turned on with quite the same readiness as it was in the 1960s.

For the Apollo mission, the 'ways' to ultimate success were through a programme approach (it was Apollo 11 that finally delivered Armstrong and Aldrin to the moon) and the creation of a collaborative organization with multiple contributors working with complete transparency and the sharing of knowledge and ideas. It was acknowledged at the start that the challenge was beyond the capabilities of a single organization.

Artemis is of a scale far greater than Apollo. It, too, is being implemented through a programme approach. To achieve this, NASA is building a coalition of partnerships with industry and academia, both in the United States and internationally. Artemis represents the execution of strategy in the grandest of scales, one with multiple projects often running simultaneously, to design, manufacture and test launch rockets, crew vehicles, landing systems, space suits, mobility platforms, terrain vehicles, lunar ground stations – the list goes on. For each project, there is the initiation, planning, execution and control. There are the risks to consider, issues and problems that will inevitably arise that are to be resolved, and decisions to be made. All on the route to completion of the task.

To boldly go...

For people to go further than they have ever been before, they will need to go for longer periods of time – and use resources they find at their destinations. They will have to overcome radiation, isolation, gravity and the most extreme of environments.

As a first step, NASA has designed an entirely new and super powerful rocket, called the Space Launch System, and a new generation human space capsule, Orion, that can support people from launch, through deep space, and back safely to Earth. Together these provide the foundation needed to send humans back to lunar orbit, and as of April 2021, they were nearing the end of testing and development.

The approach to landing and operating on the Moon is one quite different to that in the 1960s. The idea is to have lunar landers that are reusable and that can land anywhere on the lunar surface. NASA has worked out that the simplest way to do this is to have a platform in orbit, around the moon, from which to transition – an orbiting platform to act as a stopover for human capsules. It is calling this lunar outpost, Gateway – and this will sit in balance between the Earth's and Moon's gravity in a position that is ideal for launching even deeper space missions.

On later Artemis missions, crew will arrive at the Gateway aboard Orion. On the Gateway, they will be able to conduct research and take trips down to the Moon's surface. At the lunar south pole, NASA and its partners will develop a Base Camp to support longer expeditions, with a module in which the astronauts can stay, a terrain vehicle, and power systems. A LunaNet will enable robotic landers, rovers and astronauts on the Moon to communicate with a network, similar to that on Earth but with far greater reach. Rovers analysing samples can send data to relays orbiting the Moon, which can then transmit the data back to Earth. When astronauts are on the lunar surface, they will be able to receive real-time alerts of incoming solar flares from space weather instruments, giving them ample time to seek cover. LunaNet will also support positioning, navigation and timing services, allowing for more precise surface operations and science than ever before.

It was over a decade ago, in 2009, that it was discovered that the Moon contains millions of tonnes of ice. This ice can be extracted and purified for water, and be separated into oxygen for breathing and hydrogen for rocket fuel. As such, the moon is uniquely suited to prepare and propel astronauts to Mars, and beyond. This technology and methodology, NASA believes can be replicated throughout the Solar System, and represents the next chapter of human space exploration.

One man's story

With the exception of this one chapter, every story in this book has been about one remarkable individual (or sometimes two or three), who through their personal vision and sense of purpose, their commitment and hard work, have made things happen. They are inspiration for all of us to know that we have it within us to make a difference. This story is different because the vision is already defined and centrally governed and co-ordinated by the biggest space agency in the world. Nonetheless, within NASA, as well as the academic and industry partners working in collaboration, there are tens of thousands of stories of human endeavour that come together to make it happen. One such story is that of William Allen, a mechanical design engineer who has spent his entire working life, over 35 years, at NASA's Jet Propulsion Laboratory (JPL) in Pasadena, California. One of ten NASA field centres dotted across the United States, JPL is managed by the nearby California Institute of Technology and its charter is to research and develop unmanned vehicles for space exploration. In order of complexity, these are spacecraft that 'flyby' a planet, then 'orbit' it, then 'land' on a planet and finally 'rove' on the surface of a planet. The latest project that William Allen worked on was the extraordinarily sophisticated new rover, Perseverance, that we witnessed land on Mars on 18 February 2021. These robotic missions are the stepping stones for man and woman to follow in a journey to the red planet.

The vision for Mars

'Most people don't know that President Bush senior made a similar declaration to J.F Kennedy,' says Allen. On the 20th anniversary of the Apollo 11 Moon landing, in 1989, he announced plans to send humans back to the Moon 'to stay' and ultimately to send astronauts to explore Mars. The difference was the timeframe wasn't deemed critical; the important thing was to get there safely. 'That started the Mars programme, and since then we've been launching spacecraft to Mars every two years,' says Allen, adding that in the years 1998 and 1999, 'there were two mission failures in a row [Mars Climate Orbiter, then Mars Polar Lander were lost] and Congress put on the brakes, told us we had to prove we could do some basic things without incident. We have no choice but to learn from our failures, he adds, 'but it ended up a good thing. That's what formulated the two Mars exploration rovers – Spirit and Opportunity. That's how they came about.'

Allen worked on these two rovers, and then the next generation rover, Curiosity, which was much bigger, about the size of a small sports utility vehicle, before moving onto the latest rover, Perseverance. This latest rover preserves the same architecture of its predecessor but accommodates a whole news suite of instruments, as well as a processing system that is designed specifically to collect, carefully select and document the first samples of rock and regolith (broken rock and soil) from Mars, to be cached and returned to Earth on a future mission. Over the past two decades, missions flown by NASA have shown us that Mars was once very different from the cold, dry planet it is today. Photographs taken from orbiters, and early rovers, reveal a fossilized river delta preserved in sedimentary rock, and layers of rock formed from mineral salt produced from sea water as it evaporated. Water didn't just flow sporadically on Mars as had once been thought, but persistently, potentially long enough to support the development of microbial life. This new rover has technology that enabled it to safely touch down in the Jezero Crater, the site of this delta, avoiding steep cliffs and boulder fields, and also to drive autonomously with far fewer instructions from engineers on Earth than its predecessors. Its new suite of instruments includes SHERLOC (Scanning Habitable Environments with Raman & Luminescence for Organics & Chemicals) which detects organic matter and minerals, and PIXL (short for Planetary Instrument for X-ray Lithochemistry) which maps the chemical composition of rocks and sediments.

Using these instruments to read the geological history embedded in Mars's rocks will give scientists a richer sense of what the planet was like in its distant past, and could help us understand why Earth and Mars, despite some early similarities, are now so different. Importantly, this data can also help answer one of the key questions of astrobiology: Are there signs (or biosignatures) of past microbial life on Mars?

To be a part of a programme that is on the road to discovering such ground-breaking science, that will potentially change the way that we look at the universe and ourselves, is the privilege of working at JPL. 'The flip side,' says Allen, 'is that we're always under the gun. We have a launch window to Mars every two years and each mission we're taking to the next level.'

With fixed deadlines determined by the rotations of planet Earth and Mars around the Sun, naturally I was curious if deadlines were ever missed. 'Yes,' he says, in reference to the Curiosity rover. 'That was the first time in my experience that we went to NASA headquarters and Congress, and said, look, we can make the launch but here are the challenges if we do.' The spacecraft was almost completed; it was physically built but it needed further testing and development of certain subsystems. In the end it was a consensual decision to delay the launch in 2009, but the cost of doing so would have been better avoided. There wasn't the option of increasing the scope; rather they determined the minimal amount of work required to keep the project alive, reduced staffing, and completed the remainder of the work for launch in 2011.

The 'grandeur of the task'

Though highly technical and complex in nature, the implementation of a strategy to build a rover that is to be sent to Mars, requires attendance to the same universal elements of any strategy that is to be implemented, which might broadly be described as technology, methodology and the human dynamics of working together as a team.

When Allen was asked about the technology, he responded: 'We fly proven reliable technology which takes time to test and verify under harsh and extreme conditions. We've got one shot and it's got to work. By the time we test and prove something is flightworthy, there's newer technology out there that's bigger, better and faster.' That being said, they use leading-edge technology to do their jobs on the ground.

As for the methodology, there is a natural built-in framework around the launch windows every two years. It is understood what needs to be achieved in these predetermined timeframes, and there are milestones – or 'reviews' as they call them, overseen by a senior board – that people and subsystems have to meet along the way.

When it comes to human dynamics, 'We have the same challenges as any other organization,' insists Allen. 'We have all the personality types, all the different leadership styles – the good and the bad.' However, many of the frictions and challenges – from competing agendas, to the challenge of having a bunch of extremely bright and competitive people all in the same room – are put to one side because of what Allen calls 'the grandeur of the task'. There is a compelling imperative to work together. 'To credit JPL,' he says, 'it has built a culture that nurtures working together, and rewards it.'

Optimizing organization structure and processes to execute strategy

One of JPL's ways of operating, which is unusual, is that it employs what it calls Cognizant engineers – Cog Es for short. Their role is to facilitate the entire development of a spacecraft subsystem that, with other subsystems, contribute to the making of a spacecraft. They gather around them a team from specialist disciplines – design, analysis, simulation, manufacturing, testing and so on – in order to deliver the subsystem, but they are the ones who are ultimately held responsible. 'It cuts through any political and personal challenges,' says Allen. It sounds a weighty responsibility for the Cog Es but the JPL organization is built around supporting this structure. There are no witch-hunts of people when something goes wrong. Rather, the aim is to find out what went wrong (not whose error it might have been). 'And we're very thorough about it,' says Allen. 'We have a couple of methodologies for gathering lessons learned, and we put them in writing and we teach them.' It is an on-going process, so people learn from past mistakes, and continue to add to the documentation for the future.

Something else that JPL does extremely well is to respond quickly and intelligently to issues as they arise. 'We're marching towards a launch date so we can't stop the mission to figure out a problem,' says Allen. 'So, at the same time, we pull together a small team of highly-focused subject matter experts from different fields, depending what the problem is, and try to understand, figure out and solve the problem.' It's called a Tiger team. 'It's helpful to come in with an open mind, leave at the door any biases or predispositions you might have and be open to a new way of thinking, a new way of learning,' he says. 'These are not problems that exist in a book anywhere, they're typically unique.'

Solving problems 140 million miles away that you can't see or touch

'I'm still amazed at the ability of our teams to react, discover and solve the problems that we have,' he says, 'I don't know if you saw the news?' he asks, in reference to Ingenuity, a small robotic solar helicopter that hitched a lift to Mars on Perseverance and, on 19 April 2021, made the very first powered, controlled flight by an aircraft on a planet other than Earth, taking off vertically into the extremely thin atmosphere on Mars, hovering and then landing. On the first attempt, the helicopter failed to go into flight-ready mode. 'So, we're 140 million miles away. We can't see it; we can't touch it. But a team of people comes together and figures out in a day what the problem is, and then in another day finds a solution that involves flushing and installing new software from 140 million miles away. That still boggles my mind.'

I ask Allen if, when working with his team, he keeps the big Artemis vision in mind, or if his focus is on his team's piece of the jigsaw puzzle that is such an important element in making it happen. 'There's not a lot of time or room to come up for air,' he says. The design, build and testing of a rover such as Perseverance, takes brain power, commitment and a lot of hard work. 'But to see your rover touch down on another planet, that's as surreal as it gets. To think, we did that! That energizes you for the next one.'

The next project

For Allen, the next project is to design a spacecraft to collect the samples that have been gathered and cached by the Perseverance rover on the surface of Mars, and launch these samples aboard a rocket into Mars orbit. Then after that, the next project will be to design a spacecraft to collect the samples from Mars orbit and return them to Earth – where, the details still to be worked out, the samples will crash land in a landing pod in the Utah desert. 'So, it's a significant effort,' he says. 'We're working the first leg of it now and we'll launch the mission towards the end of this decade.'

Hard work the path to success

What he describes is a part of the most extraordinary journey, for Artemis, for humankind, and for Allen himself, a mechanical design engineer whose focus as a boy, at his own admission, was much more on athletics and playing stickball in the park than anything scientific. 'The best lesson of my childhood was being put to work and doing hard labour,' he says, 'it taught me I didn't want to do hard labour all my life.' And that was the motivator for him to focus on his school work and to study engineering physics at Oregon State University. His education, plus a summer job working in the mail room of Jet Propulsion Laboratory, proved the best investment of his life. 'I was willing to work hard so that wasn't an issue, but actually to just fall into something that you're passionate about, I think it's rare.'

So tell me, I ask him, when are we going to see man and woman land on Mars? 'I'm not a bookie,' is his answer, 'but I would venture to say somewhere around 2040'. A vision that once existed only in the imagination of science fiction writers is now a realizable vision in the minds of physicists, engineers and astro scientists. It has taken a huge collective effort to get this far, with NASA bringing together and co-ordinating its own centres across the United States, as well as academic and industry partners at home and internationally. But break each of these institutions and partnerships down and the component parts are people, investing time and energy, working hard, and exercising the very best of their collective intelligence to push scientific and technological boundaries, constantly coming up with creative solutions as issues arise. These people, together, are implementing a strategy of unimaginable scale that we have the opportunity to witness as humankind's journey to Mars unfolds before us in the next 20 years.

CHAPTER TWELVE

Conclusions

Reading the stories of these incredible people who have accomplished so much, it is utterly apparent that when implementing strategy, few things are one-dimensional. Just as in the example of Napoleon's failed invasion of Russia at the beginning of this book, a strategy more often than not requires the pulling together of multiple disciplines, projects and objectives to achieve a set goal or vision. The deep understanding of these multiple factors – what they are, and how they interact – is critical in order to be able to measure and thus manage the strategy, and to communicate it clearly so that everyone understands how their particular tasks and projects fit into the big picture.

Importantly, what Napoleon's example also illustrates is how catastrophically things can go wrong if one's eyes, as well as focusing on the objective, aren't also darting back and forth into one's peripheral vision, taking note of and forecasting the changing environment and circumstances and the actions of one's competitors. Never has this been so true as today, in our world of super-quick technological advancements and convergent disciplines where the rate of change is speeding up exponentially.

The stories in this book highlight common, enduring truths in the execution of strategy that transcend sector differences. They amplify the importance of some factors that we intuitively acknowledge as important, such as clarity of vision, focus and simplification, prioritization of that which is most important, the writing of a plan, and communication. What these stories also do, however, is to highlight how none of us operates in a vacuum. To survive, and thrive, we must be willing to adapt – and fast. We're to be agile. We are to have an openness of mind to let go of the old and adopt the new, to embrace new technologies and constantly acquire new skills to compete with the best. We are to be ready to pivot and seize opportunities. And if we're to lead, we can't afford just to play catch-up, but must look to the far horizon, 20 or 25 years hence, and build capacity for tomorrow, today.

This is critical both for organizations and our society as a whole, and we will look in a moment at some of the trademarks of agile organizations in more detail – how they look and feel, and the shift in mindset that is required to achieve such agility. But first, just a handful of enduring truths that shine bright in the subjects of this book.

Purpose

The first must be an absolute sense of purpose. Many of our contributors enter the fray when there is a genuine *need* for reform: a civil war, failing schools, general practice in a chronic state of ill health. It is difficult for there not to be purpose in saving lives and educating our young people. But other contributors, in situations that might be regarded as less than urgent, still nonetheless have a strong sense of purpose – to generate growth, to merge two governmental bodies, to revitalize a ballet company, to champion Nepalese climbers, to awake a traditional company to the advantages of digital technology, or to fly to Mars. Interestingly, two of our contributors who feel their sense of purpose wavering, take action in order to do something they consider really worthwhile, recognizing the importance of this for their personal motivation. In the case of Dame Helena Morrissey, this was contributing to equality in the workplace with the setting up of the 30% Club, and for Emma Bridgewater, the regeneration of a pottery.

A sense of purpose, it seems, is a strong emotional driver to energize and see things through to completion, and has very little to do with making money, even if money is a product of the process. As Emma Bridgewater says, in wishing for her brand to be future-proofed, 'it's not to do with the money; it is to do with prosperity. It is to do with the people and the pride.' Emotions are clearly not to be ignored in the successful implementation of strategy.

True to self

The second enduring truth goes hand in glove with the first – every one of our contributors is true to himself or herself. They are an embodiment of what they do, and they do what they are. It is true that William Allen wasn't at all sure what he wanted to do when he was growing up (which is the case for so many people) and that Emma Bridgewater flirted for a while with the idea of being a literary agent. For some of us the journey is longer than for others. But all know that a sense of purpose is important and in the end, all are totally committed to their work. They put in long hours and work hard – no one seems to have found a way around that yet – but in the end, because they are doing something in which they believe, it doesn't seem to matter so very much.

Perhaps Tim Brighouse summed it up when he said that he had been flattered to be asked to head up social services in Birmingham. 'But I'm not a social worker,' he said, 'I never have been, and didn't feel that I would have the authority. I'm a teacher – I always thought there's no more important job in life, because we unlock kids. A teacher is key to a civilized community and social justice.'

Clear vision through the fog
(alignment and prioritization)

When executing strategy, it is absolutely essential that the strategy be clear, focused and translated logically into short-term objectives or metrics.

Lawrence Hrebiniak, Emeritus Professor in the
Department of Management at The Wharton School
of the University of Pennsylvania

No matter the organization or the setting, there are some obstacles to success that remain the same. Military theorist Carl von Clausewitz summed it up perfectly in two words: 'fog' and 'friction'. Whether fighting on the field or managing a multinational, or even trying to juggle our personal and working lives, fog envelops us in a blanket of unknowns, uncertainty and ambiguity; and our progress is mired by a constant friction of differing views and ambitions.

In today's increasingly complex world, it is critical to be able to read the big picture and yet see a clear path to achieving one's end goal within it – to be able to prioritize, focus and intensify one's effort on the important issues. There is truth in the saying that to prioritize many things is to prioritize nothing at all. And to be able to prioritize *one* thing – the priority above all else – is a rare and valuable skill. Of all our contributors, the prize for such clarity of vision in the densest and most blinding of fogs must go to a man trained in military theory himself, General Sir Michael Rose. There is confidence and beauty in the single stroke of his metaphorical red pen, deleting the skull-busting confusion of conflicting UN Security Council resolutions in Bosnia and Herzegovina and starting again, with a replacement mission that comprised three (and only three) elements – the most important of which, very clearly, was the delivery of humanitarian aid on which so many people's lives depended.

In a three-way civil war there was inevitably massive friction too, with different UN member states holding differing views and differing political agendas, for which Rose had little time and adopted a robust approach toward. He wanted a small, committed team where the troubles were in Sarajevo, and was of the view that the number of UN personnel at the headquarters in the winter Olympic village of Kiseljak needed to be drastically reduced. It was of little relevance, then, that everybody from Kofi Annan down told him it was impossible. He thought differently – and cut off the electricity, central heating and water supply.

Prioritizing objectives for success – lessons learned from the Special Forces

One area in which an urgent pursuit of top-priority objectives is essential for a successful outcome, and from which we can learn, is Special Forces operations. Special Forces teams are typically small. The longer they are on the ground the more vulnerable they are, and thus in operations they need to be utterly focused, and fast. Time is of the essence.

Retired Admiral William McRaven carried out a retrospective analysis of over 40 Special Forces operations in US Special Operations Command. In all 40 operations there were a number of objectives to be achieved but, importantly, these objectives weren't equal in their contribution to a successful outcome. McRaven found that the common success factor was to limit the

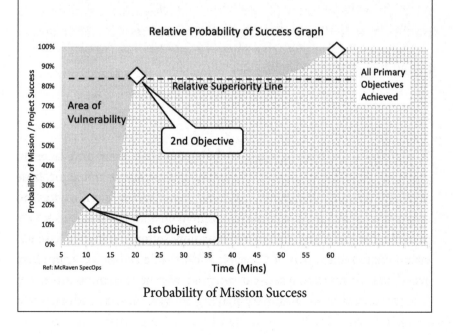

Probability of Mission Success

number of objectives as far as possible, by identifying one or two that would have the most significant impact, and pursuing them first and fast. Once these important objectives had been achieved, the vulnerability of the team on the ground lessened and a line was crossed – a line identified by McRaven as the 'line of relative superiority' – where the mission was more likely to succeed than it was to fail.

In the graph above, the probability of the mission's success is measured on the vertical axis and time is measured on the horizontal axis. The area in light grey is the area of vulnerability, where the Special Forces are most at danger. In this example, the first objective was achieved after only 10 minutes and the probability of success immediately leapt to 20 per cent. The second objective was achieved after 20 minutes and took the probability of success up to 85 per cent. At this point the vulnerability of the soldiers was radically reduced and the relative superiority line was crossed, and the mission was more likely to be successful than not. After 60 minutes, all primary objectives were achieved and the mission accomplished.

Agility

It requires a certain mindset to be agile, with your antennae on constant alert for changing circumstances, while at the same time focusing on your objective – and, perhaps, having a willingness to forgo one goal for an alternative and maybe more ambitious one. Who better as an example of someone exhibiting agility than Roald Amundsen, mentioned in the introduction of this book? Amundsen was a man with a strong sense of purpose, willing to explore unknown territories and most definitely playing to win. He was sailing north to explore the North Pole basin when he heard that Captain Scott was on his way to Antarctica, intent on being the first to reach the

South Pole – and turned his ship on a sixpence to race south. His sense of purpose was as strong as ever, and his exploratory spirit alive and well. It was just his objective that had changed – and in being agile and prepared (his team of men fit and skilled), and up to meeting a new challenge, he was the one who reached the South Pole first, forever to win his place in the annals of the heroic age of polar exploration.

Many of our contributors, too, exhibit highly agile mindsets – and arguably it is one of the most important attributes for anybody determined to make a difference in today's fast-changing world. Having a clear sense of purpose and being true to oneself is as important as it has ever been, but so too is creating one's vision of the future and acting upon it quickly. General Sir Michael Rose only had a year in office as Commander of the UN Protection Force in Bosnia and Herzegovina, and set to work as soon as there was a hint that he would be appointed the job. As a new head at Wellington College, Sir Anthony Seldon wasted no time inviting girls to join the boys at the school, making it co-ed in his first term. English National Ballet's artistic director, Tamara Rojo, insisted on four new ballet masters as a condition of her taking the job. And so it goes on.

A number of our contributors are true protagonists in the creation of what might be considered exemplary and modern agile organizations – ones that are dynamic, in that they are quick to adapt to new challenges and ways of doing things, and at the same time stable, in that they have baseline structures and processes in place to eliminate the need to reinvent the wheel and repeat work. They are, in other words, efficient – while also being innovative.

The following might be regarded a small point in the running of Emma Bridgewater's pottery business, but it is also a wonderful metaphor for an agile organization – one that is both dynamic and stable. Bridgewater's aim is that with every new collection, the customer 'entirely recognizes and feels comfortable with it and at the same time is entirely charmed by the new relevant thing'. There is both stability and dynamism in the design. In practice, this is achieved by keeping the exact same shape of mug, bowl, jug and serving dish that she designed at the very start – and coming up with new patterns to paint on these original shapes that are fresh and appealing. Now, there's a simple formula for success.

Then there are our two young employees of the Norwegian multinational oil and gas company Equinor – Jens Festervoll and Stein Petter Aannerud. To be agile, they first looked at the long horizon – the company ambition is to increase investment levels in renewable energy to between 15 and 20 per cent capital expenditure in 2030, compared with around 1 per cent at the time of writing. And then they asked the question head on: how on earth are we going to do that? The answer was to increase efficiency and reduce costs through the adoption of digital technology, and Festervoll and Aannerud created a small, agile group within the organization in order to do so.

Executing strategy

Those who want to initiate change and make a difference know that the skill lies in always looking ahead and executing strategy to time, to budget and to the best possible quality. Staying in business depends on it, and there is certainly no chance of winning – of *thriving* – without the excellent implementation of strategy. Critically, for this to be successful, operations must be aligned with the strategy. If circumstances dictate that the strategy evolves or is changed, then operations must change as well. And for a quick and nimble response, it's helpful to have highly developed organizational skills, as well as the ability to plan, brief, adapt quickly and brief again, and mobilize people to action.

A model for executing strategy

Strategy

Vision

Adapt and learn

Deliver effects

Sustaining momentum

Align and prioritise

Organise and engage

Strategy

Operations

Cascade briefing

Planning

Rhythm of execution

This strategy model illustrates the interface between strategy and operations. The two spinning discs – the top one representing strategy and the bottom one operations – can be likened to a car gearbox and clutch. Release the clutch and the two plates come together – operations link with strategy and there is traction. In a fast-changing world, issues can arise if an organization's strategy doesn't evolve to meet a change in the environment or in the market, and operations are then aligned to a strategy that is no longer relevant. Issues can also arise if a strategy evolves but the clutch is disengaged and operations continue on the old course.

Two lessons can be learned from this: first, it is crucial to repeatedly ask the question 'has the situation changed?' and to change the strategy accordingly. Second, it is important to ensure – through careful planning, briefing, adapting and learning – that the clutch remains engaged so there continues to be traction and operations remain aligned with the strategy.

In business, a distinction is often made between task-oriented leadership – where the focus is on completing the necessary tasks at hand in order to achieve a goal – and relationship-oriented leadership, where the focus is on supporting, motivating and developing people. The view of those at Skarbek on this matter is clear: echoing the words of the US army's leading expert on leadership, Colonel Dandridge M. Malone, 'the very essence of leadership is its purpose. The purpose of leadership is to accomplish a task. That is what leadership does.' However, they fully appreciate that as well as accomplishing the task – indeed, *in order* to accomplish the task – it is important to nurture and develop both the individual and the team, arguably more so today than ever before.

Whilst COVID-19 put paid to international travel, indeed to any travel at all, the trend in recent times has been for people to move wherever the best opportunities lie, sometimes to different continents. As creative knowledge and learning-based tasks become more important, organizations need a distinctive value proposition to acquire and retain the best talent. Gone are the days when the leadership view was that 'people need to be directed and managed, otherwise they won't know what to do'. And here to stay is the view that when given clear responsibility and authority, people will be engaged, they will take care of each other, and figure out solutions to deliver exceptional results. Skarbek's belief is that it is important to connect what they call the 'nervous system' of an organization to create time for people to get to know one another, to recognize, value and thank people, to empathize and to build trust – for without trust there is no cohesion. This has been more challenging when working remotely at home during the pandemic, with those who had already built bonds of trust being the winners. There is nothing that can quite replace being in the room with one's colleagues, but nonetheless project teams have long worked remotely across boundaries and time zones and COVID-19 has served to accelerate the adoption of video calls, which if used well, can be an effective way to build relationships of trust.

Communication

This brings us on to another enduring truth in the execution of strategy – communication. This came more naturally to some of our contributors than others, but all would argue that it is utterly essential for successful execution of strategy. The man who understood this better than anybody was President of GSK Consumer Healthcare, John Clarke. Clarke approached communication with characteristic thoroughness as if it were a strategy unto itself, repeatedly communicating the simplest of messages until he could be confident that everybody understood. And he was exceptionally good at the personal message, too. 'He would come to a lot of meetings,' said Dr Robbins, 'and he'd say, "if you're working on innovation, there is nothing more important for you to be working on than that." I haven't seen that too often before or since.'

Then there is communication to the wider world. At the start of Nimsdai's mission to climb all the 8,000-metre peaks, he was no expert on social media but he made it a priority to learn, and had he not done so it's unlikely he would have got the funding to complete his mission. For Emma Bridgewater, her early adoption of the Internet and social media – showing off her pretty pottery on Instagram – saved, and remarkably, grew her business through the pandemic.

Taking the initiative

Finally, let's return to our doctor, James Morrow. It might seem odd that so many lessons on executing strategy (and particularly on agile organizations) might be drawn from general practice, which is in a state of ill health across the United Kingdom. But Granta Medical Practices in Cambridgeshire is an exception, and it is so because of one man with an expansive and forward-looking mindset who is at once humble and willing to listen, and at the same time confident that it is he, together with his fellow practitioners, who are best positioned to take on board the issues at hand and come up with creative solutions. Dr Morrow looks at the far horizon – his aim is to create a structure fit for purpose for the next 50 to 70 years – and recognizes that change is inevitable; thus the question to ask is *do you want to play a part in shaping the future or not?*

Like other contributors to this book, Morrow reaches beyond his discipline of medicine and learns from beyond – introducing straightforward business principles into his practice that markedly improve flow and productivity. None of the humanity of general practice is lost. Far from it: the practice members are uncompromising about their ethos and core values of trust and mutual respect, both among themselves and with patients. At the heart of every decision made is the patient's best interests, the practitioners constantly ask of themselves the question: is this what we would want for ourselves and our families? Genuinely, proudly, they don't believe they could provide a better service to anyone who was paying for it than they are providing through the NHS; a view endorsed by consistent positive feedback from their patients and a rating of 'outstanding' from the Care Quality Commission – all without one extra penny of resource. They are on the same national contract as every other general practice in the country and, unsurprisingly, GPs are queuing up to work there.

The good news is that Granta Medical Practices is setting up a Primary Care Innovation Academy at the Judge Business School at Cambridge University to apply some business and academic analysis and rigour to what they have been doing, and to offer an executive programme for other GPs and managers as a way of disseminating some of the lessons learned. An inaugural cohort was run in 2020, and if readers of this book spread the word and encourage only a handful of GPs to sign up to this academy and learn from Granta's example, then the writing of this book will have been a worthwhile exercise. But the hope is that the book will touch and benefit many more people besides.

We live in challenging times, ever more demanding with accelerating digitalization, disruptive technologies and democratization of information. The execution of strategy is difficult, and arguably it will become more difficult still. But in the complexity and confusion, there is also opportunity and hope. Technology can be disruptive, but it can also offer seamless integration, unlock value and enable quick reactions to business needs. A winning mindset can look to the far horizon and choose to be instrumental in influencing and shaping the future. The gap between intent and delivery, between strategy and the execution thereof, can be closed. The important thing is to be agile on one's feet and build capacity for tomorrow, today.

Rhythm of execution

Just as a drummer on a dragon boat sets the tempo for the paddlers, so the length and frequency of meetings sets the tempo for the implementation of a project plan. Any regular attendee of meetings will understand the danger of this – more meetings can very easily mean more chat and less doing. But this trap can easily be avoided by ensuring the drum is beating at just the right pace depending on the phase of operations. At the start, for instance, a fast rhythm – a 10-minute stand-up meeting every day – can set the tone for the speed of the operations and the discipline needed to deliver. Then a steadier rhythm can be established as the project gets underway, with key decision-making meetings scheduled in, as well as shorter meetings to check progress and priorities moving forward (not forgetting to have a brief congratulatory glance over the shoulder as well). Then, if at any time an issue requiring urgent attention arises, the drumbeat can be sped up again.

Naturally, issues will arise – and decisions will need to be taken. The handling of such issues and decisions are the two greatest determinants of the speed of a project, and it's good to be prepared for the unavoidable. One approach might be to quickly assemble an emergency team – a Tiger team, as we saw at NASA's Jet Propulsion Laboratory – that is only formed in order to resolve a particular issue, before it is dissolved and the people in it moved back to their original roles.

Planning

What is the aim? What are the factors to be considered? And what are the options? From these three simple questions, a plan can be devised. Planning involves stepping back from the day-to-day operations and asking where the business is headed and what are its priorities. It has generally been regarded as a management process – looking at a sequence of events in time and space, estimated costs, allocation of resources and so on – but it can also be a creative one.

A useful metaphor to illustrate this case is the architect and the structural engineer. An architect doesn't dive straight into the detail, but starts with a sketch, some drawings and possibly paintings. An architect will usually come up with several artistic designs from which a choice can be made depending on aesthetic appeal, the practicalities of the budget and the functional specifications of the job. And here lies the first secret of good planning – the consideration of alternatives. Such is the tempo and pressure of organizations today that the temptation can be to jump straight to the first available solution without considering the options. Indeed, the more experienced the manager, the more likely this is to happen; often rewarded for being bright, quick-thinking and able, there is the danger that he or she might fall back on heuristics: mental shortcuts resulting from years of experience, which discourage someone from taking the time to look for alternatives.

This is a mistake. It is very easy to have false starts in planning if we're not clear about what we are aiming to achieve and the very best way of achieving it – and time dedicated to working this out at the start of a project is always worthwhile. Paul Heugh describes an occasion when, having found one solution to a problem, he invited everybody in his team to metaphorically put cold towels around their heads and ask, 'what other ways are there to achieve this plan? How would Superman do it? How would Mother Teresa do it? Or Gandhi?' By putting themselves mentally into a completely different space and looking at the problem from a different point of view, they knocked months off one particular project.

Then, and only then, can the chosen solution be translated into a project plan, just as an architectural design is translated into engineering drawings and a sequence of building activities – thus combining the creative design process with the management process. Injecting creativity into the planning session in this manner not only throws up alternative and often better solutions; it also generates a different response from those involved. It awakens those who might otherwise regard a management exercise as a bit of a chore. It's more engaging.

Ability is what you are capable of, motivation determines what you do, and attitude determines how well you do it.

Lou Holtz, former American football player, coach and analyst

The engagement of those involved in delivering a project is of course a critical factor in the successful execution of a strategy. Few people like or even accept commands handed down from above; quite rightly they want to feel involved and for their contribution to be valued. They want to feel a part of what is going on. For this, Skarbek strongly advocates a fully integrated planning session, that might take a couple of days. Ideally, everybody working on a project should be brought together under one roof, regardless of the depth or longevity of his or her involvement. In a global organization this will involve flying people in from around the world with all the associated costs. During the COVID-19 pandemic, of course, this hasn't been possible. There are now remarkably good software platforms that can bring everybody on a team together in a simulated meeting room on screen, allowing everyone to see where a new initiative sits in an organization's overall strategy, and encouraging people to be involved and to feel ownership of a project, and responsibility for its success. The software platforms are a wonderful addition to an organization's armoury, but still, nothing quite replaces the creative energy that is sparked when people are gathered together, and this is something still worth investing in where possible.

In addition to thinking through the alternatives (as described above), Skarbek incorporates a number of different approaches to its integrated planning sessions, which might appear obvious when spelled out but are nonetheless frequently ignored (or not even considered) in planning.

1) Planning in the traditional project management sense of the word, which emerged from the engineering sector, commonly refers to the 'dictionary of deliverables'. The first question asked is, *what are the end products of the project?* And these can be broken down, and broken down again, into components. So the product might be a bridge, for example, or a spacecraft or a car. Break down the car and one component is the engine. Break down the engine and you have a crankshaft, pistons, valves, spark plugs and fans. By breaking down the structure into its component parts, each can be looked at individually, and a plan made.

   The question this traditional approach doesn't ask, however, and which is of great importance, is *what is the effect that we want to achieve?* This can apply both to potential sponsors within a company and the consumer. Those in the marketing business have long understood how human behaviour effects consumerism, and this response of the human to the product or service is just as valid as the product or service itself, and should be factored into the planning at the start. Does it make the consumer feel excited, or environmentally responsible, or satisfied to have purchased something of rarity and value?

2) Traditionally, planning involves the mapping of activities and tasks: what needs to be done and in what order. Some activities can be done in parallel, others sequentially. It's important to understand how long tasks will take and what resources will be needed. But another factor, essential for any activity and yet commonly overlooked in the

planning, is the *information* required to undertake a task, and the dissemination of that information to the key players undertaking the task.

One way to help plan the gathering and flow of information to the right place at the right time is to visualize a double helix with two strands winding around each other like a twisted ladder. In an integrated planning session, time and effort would be taken to organize the activities and tasks on one strand of the double helix and, importantly, the information required for those tasks and activities to be undertaken on the second strand of the double helix, with the rungs of the twisted ladder representing the path along which the information would flow. In practice, attention needs to be paid to the dissemination of information as much as to the gathering of the information itself, which means crystal-clear signalling of information (many a message is lost in poorly constructed emails received by overly busy recipients). The importance of this can't be overstated. Projects can only proceed at the pace that information is gathered and sent to those undertaking the task – and failure to do so is one of the main reasons for projects running over time and budget.

3) Remember those who are to make the decisions. People's diaries are busy; it's common for them to fill up four to six weeks ahead. In which case it is important, at the integrated planning session, to identify the points at which key decisions are to be made and lock dates in the diary well in advance for stakeholders to attend key decision-making meetings – and ensure all the information needed to make the decision is gathered in good time. Leave the scheduling of meetings to the last minute and the chances are that you will be obliged to wait three or four weeks for a decision to be made, and a high price will be paid in lost time, energy and focus.

For everybody on a new initiative to meet together under the same roof allows people to spend time together, to put faces to names (particularly important for global projects operating across continents) and, importantly, to understand everybody's roles and specific responsibilities – that's not just *their own* roles and responsibilities, but *other people's* roles and responsibilities as well. All evidence suggests that clarity around roles and responsibilities is the feature of an organization most correlated to speed of operations, stability and – when issues arise, or when there's a change in the environment or the markets – agility to adapt accordingly.

All of us at Skarbek hope very much that you have enjoyed this book and found lessons in it that you might be able to adapt to your own personal and professional life. The content draws on years of the team's collective experience of managing projects and making things happen. Skarbek is well-versed in the methodology and technology to streamline processes, the organization, mobilization, planning and execution required to implement strategy. But at its heart, we all understand that the differentiating factor in implementing any strategy is the team, the people and the dynamics between them. Here we have scribed the stories of exemplars in making things happen who inspire us, and we hope, inspire you – to know that every one of us has it within us to make a difference.

Index